The Law of Interrogations and Confessions

A Guide for Law Enforcement Officers
and
Students of Law and Justice

Henry F. Fradella

The Law of Interrogations and Confessions

A Guide for Law Enforcement Officers and Students of Law and Justice

Henry F. Fradella, J.D., Ph.D.

W. B. Sheridan Law Books

Academica Press
Washington ~ London

Library of Congress Cataloging-in-Publication Data

Names: Fradella, Henry F. (author)
Title: The law of interrogations and confessions : a guide for law enforcement officers and students of law and justice | Fradella, Henry F.
Description: Washington : Academica Press, 2024. | Includes references.
Identifiers: LCCN 2024934388 | ISBN 9781680533439 (hardcover) | 9781680533446 (e-book)

Acknowledgments

This monograph represents an updating and expansion of what was a single book chapter in a book entitled *Criminal Procedure for the Criminal Justice Professional*. That book was originally written by John N. Ferdico published by West Publishing in 1975 as *Criminal Procedure for the Law Enforcement Officer*. I had the honor of becoming a coauthor on the book when it was in its tenth edition, published in 2009. I restructured the chapter on interrogations and confessions and kept it up-to-date through the publication of the twelfth edition of the book in 2016. The book went out of print with that edition and the copyright, therefore, reverted to the authors. I had not intended to do anything with the material until a few members of law enforcement reached out to me and asked for a resource to help them navigate the ever-changing legal landscape of constitutional criminal procedure, generally, and with the law of interrogations and confessions, specifically. I hope this book fills helps to fill that void. I am grateful to the contributions of John N. Ferdico and Christopher D. Totten, both of whom were my coauthors in earlier iterations of the materials presented in this monograph.

Contents

Chapter 1:
Introduction **1**

Chapter 2:
The Due Process Voluntariness Approach **5**

Chapter 3:
The Short-Lived "Focus of the Investigation Test **13**

Chapter 4:
The Per Se Approach of *Miranda v. Arizona* **17**

A. *Miranda*'s Limitation to Testimonial Evidence 24

B. The Impact of *Miranda* 26

Chapter 5:
Voluntariness and Due Process After *Miranda* **31**

A. Physical Force 31

B. Psychological Coercion by Police and Its Effect on Voluntariness 32

C. Practices That Do Not Violate Due Process 33

D. The Effect of Particular Personal Characteristics of Suspects on Voluntariness 44

Chapter 6:
When Does *Miranda* Apply? **47**

A. Custody 47

B. Interrogation 64

C. Assertion of *Miranda* Rights Must Be Clear and Unambiguous 86

D. Silence Insufficient to Invoke Rights *Prior to* Custodial Interrogation 89

Chapter 7:
Giving *Miranda* Warnings **93**

A. Sufficiency of the Language Used in *Miranda* Warnings 93

B. Manner in Which Law Enforcement Administers Warnings 95

C. Timing of Warnings 95

Chapter 8:
Multiple Interrogations **99**

A. Attempts to Interrogate After an Unwarned Admission 99

B. Attempts to Interrogate After Right to Silence Is Invoked 104

C. Attempts to Interrogate After Right to Counsel Is Invoked 106

Chapter 9:
Waiver of *Miranda* Rights **119**

A. Express Versus Implied Waivers 120

B. The Requirements for Valid Waivers of *Miranda* Rights 132

C. Effect of *Miranda–Edwards* in Court 142

Chapter 10:
Interrogation and the Sixth Amendment **151**

A. Attachment of Sixth Amendment Right to Counsel 151

B. Fifth Amendment "Interrogation"
Versus Sixth Amendment "Deliberate Elicitation 154

C. Waiver of Sixth Amendment Right to Counsel 162

Chapter 11:
Conclusion **169**

A. Summary of "Black Letter Law" 169

B. Concluding Thoughts 171

Bibliography **173**

Index **193**

List of Tables and Figures

Table 1: Interrogation Tactics That Violate Due Process **34**

Table 2: The Role of Location in Determining Custody **54**

Figure 1: *Miranda* Waiver Form **122**

Table 3: Stages of Criminal Cases **153**

Chapter 1:

Introduction

The Fifth Amendment's Self-Incrimination Clause guarantees that no person "shall be compelled in any criminal case to be a witness against himself." This so-called negative right gained international prominence as a result of the U.S. Supreme Court's landmark decision in *Miranda v. Arizona*, a case that radically changed Fifth Amendment jurisprudence concerning criminal interrogations, admissions, and confessions.[1]

The Self-Incrimination Clause also applies in settings other than those covered by *Miranda*. For example, barring grants of immunity, witnesses and targets alike may invoke the privilege during grand jury proceedings. Similarly, those called to testify before congressional or other governmental hearings may also refuse to answer questions if their responses would tend to incriminate themselves unless they, too, have been granted immunity. This book, though, focuses on the law governing statements that criminal justice professionals commonly take from criminal suspects or defendants.

The terms *statement*, *admission*, *interrogation*, and *confession* are used throughout this book.

- **Statement** is a broad term meaning simply any oral or written declaration or assertion.

- **Admission** means a person's statement or acknowledgment of facts tending to incriminate that person, but not sufficient of itself to establish guilt of a crime. An admission, alone or in connection with other facts, tends to show the existence of one or more, but not all, elements of a crime. For example, suspects often admit

---

1 Miranda v. Arizona, 384 U.S. 436 (1966).

that they were present at the scene of a crime but deny that they committed the crime.

- An **interrogation** is the process through which law enforcement officials pose questions or engage in other activities that are the functional equivalent of asking direct questions to someone whom they suspect is involved in criminal activity.
- A **confession** means a person's statement or acknowledgment of facts establishing that person's guilt of all elements of a crime.

There are several approaches taken to safeguarding constitutional rights in the interrogation context.

1. The Due Process Clauses of the Fifth and Fourteenth Amendments guarantee that any and all statements, admissions, and confessions to be introduced against a criminal defendant at trial be voluntary. Chapter 2 explores this approach in detail. Chapter 5 then returns to the concept of voluntariness as it intersects with the framework established by the U.S. Supreme Court in *Miranda v. Arizona.* [2]
2. The "focus-of-the-investigation" text was a short-lived approach to protecting the constitutional rights of the accused during interrogations. Although this approach was largely replaced by later developments, it is summarized in Chapter 3 primarily for historical context.
3. The Self-Incrimination Clause of the Fifth Amendment guarantees that any and all statements, admissions, and confessions that are a product of custodial interrogation cannot be introduced against a criminal defendant at trial unless certain procedural warnings (known as *Miranda* rights) were given to the person prior to the onset of custodial interrogation. Chapters 5 through 9 explain the *Miranda* decision and its contours as they evolved over the decades.

---

[2] *Id.*

4. The Right to Counsel Clause of the Sixth Amendment protects criminal defendants from making statements, admissions, or confessions without the presence and effective assistance of counsel after the initiation of formal criminal proceedings. Chapter 11 focuses on this approach.

Chapter 2:

The Due Process Voluntariness Approach

Early English common law recognized out-of-court confessions to be weak evidence. Sir William Blackstone, the English legal commentator and scholar, wrote that such confessions were "the weakest and most suspicious of all testimony; even liable to be obtained by artifice, false hopes, promises of favor, or menaces; seldom remembered accurately, or reported with due precision; and incapable in their nature of being disproved by other negative evidence."[3] Since that time, the law has always been concerned with the due process implications of confessions.

Suspicion of confessions obtained as a result of police interrogations waned for a period of time in U.S. history, but it resurfaced in the 1930s as courts began to take note of the often brutal police tactics that were used against criminal suspects.[4] In fact, the Wickersham Commission, a federal commission set up to investigate police conduct in the early 1930s, used the term *the third degree* to describe police tactics at the time.[5] They defined the term as "methods which inflict suffering, physical or mental, upon a person to obtain information about a crime."[6]

---

3 William Blackstone, Commentaries on the Laws of England 357 (1765).

4 Steven Penney, *Theories of Confession Admissibility: A Historical View*, 25 Am. J. Crim. L. 309, 332–41 (1998).

5 *Id.* at 336–37 (citing George W. Wickersham, Henry W. Anderson, Newton D. Balcer, Ada L. Comstock, William I. Grubb, William S. Kenyon, Monte M. Lemann, Frank J. Loesch, Kenneth Macintosh, Paul J. McCormick & Roscoe Pound, U.S. Nat'l Comm'n on Law Observance & Enf't, Pub. No. 11, Report on Lawlessness in Law Enforcement (1931) [hereinafter Wickersham Rep.], https://www.ojp.gov/pdffiles1/Digitization/44549NCJRS.pdf [https://perma.cc/6T7G-L3HZ].

6 Wickersham Rep., *supra* note 5, at 19.

> [T]he Commission documented the use of a litany of sadistic practices, including beating with fists, blackjacks, rubber hoses, and telephone books; the use of hot lights; confinement in airless and fetid rooms; and hanging from windows. The Commission was also concerned with psychologically abusive tactics, such as *incommunicado* detention, prolonged relay questioning, stripping the suspect of clothing, and the deprivation of sleep and food.[7]

The Wickersham Commission's report facilitated widespread change in policing in the United States. The report not only set in motion many efforts to stop police corruption and brutality but also affected the decision-making of the U.S. Supreme Court.[8] Indeed, the Court began to cite the Wickersham Commission's report on police brutality in obtaining confessions as evidence that confessions were often involuntary or unreliable.[9]

The landmark case excluding confessions on constitutional grounds was *Bram v. United States.*[10] *Bram* marked the first time the U.S. Supreme Court relied on the Fifth Amendment privilege against self-incrimination as a basis for holding that confessions had to be made voluntarily. In the years following *Bram*, however, the Court turned to the Due Process Clauses of the Fifth and Fourteenth Amendments as a justification for excluding confessions that were not voluntarily given. Under this approach, exemplified in *Brown v. Mississippi*, the "totality of the

---

7 Penney, *supra* note 4, at 336; *see also* WICKERSHAM REP., *supra* note 5, at 38–172.

8 *See, e.g.*, JEROME H. SKOLNICK & JAMES J. FYFE, ABOVE THE LAW: POLICE AND THE EXCESSIVE USE OF FORCE 47–52 (1993); Penney, *supra* note 4, at 336–37 ("The Wickersham Commission report influenced a generation of criminal justice reformers. Progressive politicians, police chiefs, and lawyers decried the persistence of the third degree and took various measures to restrain the corruption and brutality of police departments. The Supreme Court played a significant role in this campaign, citing the Wickersham Report a number of times in its post-*Brown* confessions cases." (internal citations omitted)).

9 Penney, *supra* note 4, at 336 n.149 (citing Miranda v. Arizona, 384 U.S. 436, 445 & n.5 (1966); Culombe v. Connecticut, 367 U.S. 568, 572–76 (1961); Haley v. Ohio, 332 U.S. 596, 605–06 (1944) (Frankfurter, J., concurring); Stein v. New York, 346 U.S. 156, 201–02 & n.* (1953) (Frankfurter, J., dissenting); Ashcraft v. Tennessee, 322 U.S. 143, 150 nn.5–6, 153 n.8 (1944); Chambers v. Florida, 309 U.S. 227, 238 n.11, 240 n.15 (1940)).

10 Bram v. United States, 168 U.S. 532 (1897).

circumstances" of each confession had to be examined to determine both the *voluntariness* of a confession and its overall reliability.[11]

Brown v. Mississippi concerned a case in which "several African-American defendants confessed to murder charges only after having been beaten and tortured by the local sheriff acting in conjunction with an angry white mob. The confessions were the sole evidence used against the *Brown* defendants to secure their convictions."[12] In reversing the defendants' convictions, the U.S. Supreme Court reaffirmed that confessions beaten out of suspects were inadmissible because they were involuntary, just as they had been under *Bram*; but rather than relying on the Fifth Amendment, as it had in *Bram*, the Court relied on due process principles in *Brown*.

The U.S. Supreme Court did not limit its due process approach to voluntariness to cases in which defendants were physically brutalized. The Court recognized that psychological tactics could also cause a suspect to make involuntary statements. In *Chambers v. Florida*, for example, police indiscriminately made warrantless arrests of up to forty Black men after a nighttime murder of an elderly White man.[13] There was conflicting evidence about whether the men were subjected to violence, but it was undisputed that over the course of a week, they were held in custody *incommunicado* during which police subjected them to relay questioning and threatened them with exposure to mob violence at the hands of community members angered by the killing. The Court summarized the key facts by saying:

> [The men] were led one at a time from their cells to the questioning room, quizzed, and returned to their cells to await another turn. So far as appears, the prisoners at no time during the week were permitted to see or confer with counsel or a single friend or relative. When carried singly from his cell and subjected to questioning, each found himself, a single prisoner, surrounded in a fourth-floor jail room by four to ten men, the

---

[11] Brown v. Mississippi, 297 U.S. 278 (1936).

[12] Mark A. Godsey, *Rethinking the Involuntary Confession Rule: Toward a Workable Test for Identifying Compelled Self-Incrimination*, 93 CALIF. L. REV. 465, 488 (2005) (citing *Brown*, 297 U.S. at 279).

[13] *Chambers*, 309 U.S. at 227.

> county sheriff, his deputies, a convict guard, and other white officers and citizens of the community.[14]

Despite these conditions, "five days of continued questioning had elicited no confession."[15] Then, "in hopeless desperation and fear [for] their lives," four men who had been questioned all night long confessed in hours "just after daylight."[16] Citing the Wickersham Commission's report, the Court remarked that those "who have suffered most from secret and dictatorial proceedings have almost always been the poor, the ignorant, the numerically weak, the friendless, and the powerless."[17] The Court then went on to overturn the men's convictions, reasoning as follows:

> Here, the record . . . shows, without conflict, the dragnet methods of arrest on suspicion without [a] warrant, and the protracted questioning and cross-questioning of these ignorant young colored tenant farmers by State officers and other white citizens, in a fourth-floor jail room, where as prisoners they were without friends, advisers or counselors, and under circumstances calculated to break the strongest nerves and the stoutest resistance. Just as our decision in *Brown v. State of Mississippi* was based upon the fact that the confessions were the result of compulsion, so in the present case, the admitted practices were such as to justify the statement that [t]he undisputed facts showed that compulsion was applied.[18]

Law professor Steven Penney chronicled several cases decided soon after *Chambers* in which the Court overturned the convictions of Black defendants who had been subjected to "protracted, *incommunicado* interrogations."[19] ***Incommunicado* interrogation** refers to the questioning of a person cut off from the rest of the world in a police-dominated atmosphere. In one of the important post-*Chambers* cases, *Lisenba v.*

---

14 *Id.* at 231.

15 *Id.*

16 *Id.*

17 *Id.* at 238 (citing WICKERSHAM REP., *supra* note 5, at 159).

18 *Id.* at 238–39 (internal quotations and citations omitted).

19 Penney, *supra* note 4, at 338 (citing Lomax v. Texas, 313 U.S. 544 (1941) (per curiam); Vernon v. Alabama, 313 U.S. 547 (1941) (per curiam); Canty v. Alabama, 309 U.S. 629 (1940) (per curiam); White v. Texas, 309 U.S. 631 (1940) (per curiam)).

California, the Court emphasized that a due process approach to interrogations aims to both "exclude presumptively false evidence, [as well as] to prevent fundamental unfairness in the use of evidence, whether true or false."[20] Subsequent cases emphasized that due process also concerns self-determination.[21] This is particularly evident in the plurality decision in *Watts v. Indiana*, a case in which police subjected the defendant to relay questioning over the course of a week during which time they kept in solitary confinement and deprived him of food and sleep.[22] In overturning his conviction, the Court stated:

> A confession by which life becomes forfeit must be the expression of free choice. A statement to be voluntary of course need not be volunteered. But if it is the product of sustained pressure by the police it does not issue from a free choice. When a suspect speaks because he is overborne, it is immaterial whether he has been subjected to a physical or a mental ordeal.[23]

In the 1961 case of *Rogers v. Richmond*, the Supreme Court summarized the various reasons for insisting that statements from suspects subjected to police interrogations satisfy due process notions of fundamental fairness.[24] *Rogers* reversed a murder conviction on the grounds that the defendant confessed because his will was overborne by a threat to take his wife, who suffered from significant arthritis, into custody:

> [C]onvictions following the admission into evidence of confessions which are involuntary, i.e., the product of coercion, either physical or psychological, cannot stand. This is so not because such confessions are unlikely to be true but because the methods used to extract them offend an underlying principle in the enforcement of our criminal law: that ours is an accusatorial and not an inquisitorial system—a system in which the State must establish guilt by evidence independently and freely secured and may not by coercion prove its charge against an accused out of his

---

20 *Id.* at 339 (quoting Lisenba v. California, 314 U.S. 219, 231–32 (1941)).

21 *Id.* at 343–44 (citing Haley v. Ohio, 332 U.S. 596 (1948) (plurality opinion); Malinski v. New York, 324 U.S. 401 (1945); Ashcraft v. Tennessee, 322 U.S. 143 (1944)).

22 Watts v. Indiana, 338 U.S. 49 (1949) (plurality opinion).

23 *Id.* at 53.

24 Rogers v. Richmond, 365 U.S. 534, 536 (1961).

> own mouth. . . . To be sure, confessions cruelly extorted may be and have been, to an unascertained extent, found to be untrustworthy. But the constitutional principle of excluding confessions that are not voluntary does not rest on this consideration. Indeed, in many of the cases in which the command of the Due Process Clause has compelled us to reverse state convictions involving the use of confessions obtained by impermissible methods, independent corroborating evidence left little doubt of the truth of what the defendant had confessed. Despite such verification, confessions were found to be the product of constitutionally impermissible methods in their inducement. Since a defendant had been subjected to pressures to which, under our accusatorial system, an accused should not be subjected, we were constrained to find that the procedures leading to his conviction had failed to afford him that due process of law which the Fourteenth Amendment guarantees.[25]

To summarize, then, under the due process approach, involuntary statements are unconstitutional for a number of related reasons:

1. Involuntary statements are inherently untrustworthy and unreliable; convictions based on unreliable evidence violate due process.
2. Coercive police practices are a violation of "fundamental fairness," an essential element of due process. Therefore, a confession coerced by the police violates due process, even if that confession is otherwise reliable.
3. Free choice is an essential aspect of due process; an involuntary confession cannot be the product of a person's free and rational choice.
4. Our system of justice requires the prosecution to establish guilt beyond a reasonable doubt using evidence that is constitutionally obtained.[26]

To this day, statements must still be voluntary to satisfy due process. Nonetheless, by the 1960s, the U.S. Supreme Court had taken note that the

---

[25] *Id.* at 540–41.

[26] *See generally* Gerald M. Caplan, *Questioning* Miranda, 38 VAND. L. REV. 1417, 1428–30 (1985) (surveying cases in which the U.S. Supreme Court questioned the reliability of coerced statements).

application of the voluntariness standard often proved to be "politically malleable" in practice.[27]

> Moreover, the Court failed to penetrate the secrecy of the interrogation process. Courts were constantly faced with having to resolve conflicts in testimony between police and defendants. The Supreme Court repeatedly lamented the fact that such swearing contests were almost always resolved in the police's favor. The voluntariness standard, however, offered nothing to remedy the problem. As a result, there was little evidence that the Court's decisions were having much of an effect on either lower courts or the police.[28]

The Court, therefore, began to experiment with other approaches to interrogations.

---

27 Penney, *supra* note 4, at 361.

28 *Id.* at 361–62 (internal citations omitted).

Chapter 3:

The Short-Lived "Focus of the Investigation Test

In 1964, the U.S. Supreme Court decided *Escobedo v. Illinois.*[29] The suspect in *Escobedo* had been arrested, but not indicted or arraigned—a fact that, as will be subsequently explored in Chapter 10, is highly relevant for Sixth Amendment purposes. He asked to see his lawyer, but the police denied that request and continued to interrogate him. Indeed, they falsely told him that his lawyer "didn't want to see him" even though the attorney had come to see the defendant and the police had turned him away.[30] This fact was central to the Court's decision to overturn his conviction:

> The interrogation here was conducted before petitioner was formally indicted. But in the context of this case, that fact should make no difference. When petitioner requested, and was denied, an opportunity to consult with his lawyer, the investigation had ceased to be a general investigation of an unsolved crime. Petitioner had become the accused, and the purpose of the interrogation was to "get him" to confess his guilt despite his constitutional right not to do so. At the time of his arrest and throughout the course of the interrogation, the police told petitioner that they had convincing evidence that he had fired the fatal shots. Without informing him of his absolute right to remain silent in the face of this accusation, the police urged him to make a statement.[31]

The Court went on to hold the following:

---

29 Escobedo v. Illinois, 378 U.S. 478 (1964).

30 *Id.* at 480–81.

31 *Id.* at 485.

> [W]here, as here, the investigation is no longer a general inquiry into an unsolved crime but has begun to focus on a particular suspect, the suspect has been taken into police custody, the police carry out a process of interrogations that lends itself to eliciting incriminating statements, the suspect has requested and been denied an opportunity to consult with his lawyer, and the police have not effectively warned him of his absolute constitutional right to remain silent, the accused has been denied "The Assistance of Counsel" in violation of the Sixth Amendment to the Constitution . . . and that no statement elicited by the police during the interrogation may be used against him at a criminal trial. [32]

Note that *Escobedo* did not alter the voluntariness test that had already existed to help achieve the Fifth and Fourteenth Amendment's guarantees of due process. Rather, the case added another constitutional dimension to the law of interrogations by holding that the Sixth Amendment right to counsel offered protection during pre-indictment interrogations because the "right to use counsel at the formal trial would be a very hollow thing if, for all practical purposes, the conviction is already assured by pretrial examination."[33]

Unlike the voluntariness test, *Escobedo* did not employ a totality-of-the-circumstances approach. Instead, it took one circumstance and made it the single determinative factor in all cases in which it occurred. The Court said that "when the process shifts from investigatory to accusatory—when its focus is on the accused and its purpose is to elicit a confession . . . the accused must be permitted to consult with his lawyer."[34] This came to be known as the *Escobedo* "focus of investigation test."

Escobedo is more interesting for its rationale than it is for any precedential value. It embraced the notion that the Sixth Amendment's right to counsel had relevance in stages of criminal prosecutions before trial. In doing so, it is firmly grounded in the notion of self-determination insofar as "[m]andating the presence of counsel in the interrogation room goes a long way toward ensuring that defendants will not be induced to

---

32 *Id.* at 490–91 (internal citations omitted).

33 *Id.* at 487 (internal quotations and alterations omitted).

34 *Id.* at 492.

make admissions that they would not otherwise have made."[35] Notably, *Escobedo* was decided on the heels of the Supreme Court's decision in *Gideon v. Wainwright*, in which it held that the Fourteenth Amendment's Due Process Clause incorporated the Sixth Amendment right to counsel, thereby making it applicable to the states.[36] But *Escobedo*'s "focus of the investigation test" became largely irrelevant in the wake of *Miranda v. Arizona*'s ruling regarding custodial interrogations, which, as will soon be discussed, focused on the Fifth Amendment's Self-Incrimination Clause. Still, *Escobedo* established the notion that the Sixth Amendment also has a role in "shield[ing] the individual, after formal accusation, from the more knowledgeable and skilled forces of the prosecution."[37]

---

35 Penney, *supra* note 4, at 364.

36 Gideon v. Wainwright, 372 U.S. 335 (1963).

37 Ralph Ruebner, *Police Interrogation: The Privilege Against Self-Incrimination, the Right to Counsel, and the Incomplete Metamorphosis of Justice White*, 48 U. MIAMI L. REV. 511, 545 (1994).

Chapter 4:

The Per Se Approach of *Miranda v. Arizona*

A mere two years after *Escobedo* was decided, the U.S. Supreme Court shifted its approach to confessions yet again, this time focusing on the Fifth Amendment's privilege against self-incrimination. In the landmark decision of *Miranda v. Arizona*, the Court recognized that custodial interrogations, by their very nature, generate "compelling pressures which work to undermine the individual's will to resist and to compel him to speak where he would not otherwise do so freely."[38]

The U.S. Supreme Court's opinion in *Miranda v. Arizona* encompassed three other cases, all of which dealt with the admissibility of statements obtained from a person subjected to custodial police interrogation. All four cases shared the features of ***incommunicado* interrogation**—questioning of a person cut off from the rest of the world in a police-dominated atmosphere—resulting in self-incriminating statements without ever having been warned of constitutional rights.

The Court framed its decision in *Miranda* against the backdrop of police violence and "third-degree" tactics that flourished at that time of the Wickersham Commission report that a series of studies also addressed.[39]

> In a series of cases decided by this Court long after these studies, the police resorted to physical brutality—beating, hanging, whipping—and

---

[38] Miranda v. Arizona, 384 U.S. 436, 467–68 (1966).

[39] *Id.* at 445 n.5 (citing WICKERSHAM REP., *supra* note 5, *passim*; Bates Booth, *Confessions, and Methods Employed in Procuring Them*, 4 S. CALIF. L. REV. 83 (1930); Caleb Foote, *Law and Police Practice: Safeguards in the Law of Arrest*, 52 NW. U. L. REV. 16 (1957); Jerome Hall, *The Law of Arrest in Relation to Contemporary Social Problems*, 3 U. CHI. L. REV. 345 (1936); Paul G. Kauper, *Judicial Examination of the Accused – A Remedy for the Third Degree*, 30 MICH. L. REV. 1224 (1932)).

> to sustained and protracted questioning *incommunicado* in order to extort confessions. The Commission on Civil Rights in 1961 found much evidence to indicate that "some policemen still resort to physical force to obtain confessions. . . ." The use of physical brutality and violence is not, unfortunately, relegated to the past or to any part of the country. Only recently in Kings County, New York, the police brutally beat, kicked and placed lighted cigarette butts on the back of a potential witness under interrogation for the purpose of securing a statement incriminating a third party.
>
> The examples given above are undoubtedly the exception now, but they are sufficiently widespread to be the object of concern. Unless a proper limitation upon custodial interrogation is achieved—such as these decisions will advance—there can be no assurance that practices of this nature will be eradicated in the foreseeable future.[40]

The Court emphasized that the then-current "practice of in-custody interrogation [was] psychologically, rather than physically, oriented."[41] It, therefore, devoted a large part of the *Miranda* decision—six full pages, reproduced below, to summarizing the psychological tactics that police used during custodial interrogations by discussing several of the leading policing manuals used to train interrogators:

> The officers are told by the manuals that the
>
>> principal psychological factor contributing to a successful interrogation is privacy—being alone with the person under interrogation.

---

40 *Id.* at 446–47 (quoting 5 JOHN A. HANNAH, ROBERT G. STOREY, ERWIN N. GRISWOLD, THEODORE M. HESBURGH, ROBERT S. RANKIN & SPOTTSWOOD W. ROBINSON, III, 1961 COMMISSION ON CIVIL RIGHTS REPORT: JUSTICE 17 (1961); discussing People v. Portelli, 205 N.E.2d 857 (N.Y. 1965); and citing generally, *inter alia*, Leyra v. Denno, 347 U.S. 556 (1954); Malinski v. New York, 324 U.S. 401 (1945); Ashcraft v. Tennessee, 322 U.S. 143 (1944); Ward v. Texas, 316 U.S. 547 (1942); Vernon v. Alabama, 313 U.S. 547 (1941); White v. Texas, 310 U.S. 530 (1940); Canty v. Alabama, 309 U.S. 629 (1940); Chambers v. Florida, 309 U.S. 227 (1940) ; Brown v. Mississippi, 297 U.S. 278 (1936); Wakat v. Harlib, 253 F.2d 59 (7th Cir. 1958); People v. Matlock, 336 P.2d 505 (Cal. 1959); Bruner v. People, 156 P.2d 111 (Colo. 1945); People v. Wakat, 114 N.E.2d 706 (Ill. 1953); Kier v. State, 132 A.2d 494 (Md. 1957)).

41 *Id.* at 448.

The efficacy of this tactic has been explained as follows:

> If at all practicable, the interrogation should take place in the investigator's office or at least in a room of his own choice. The subject should be deprived of every psychological advantage. In his own home, he may be confident, indignant, or recalcitrant. He is more keenly aware of his rights and more reluctant to tell of his indiscretions or criminal behavior within the walls of his home. Moreover, his family and other friends are nearby, their presence lending moral support. In his own office, the investigator possesses all the advantages. The atmosphere suggests the invincibility of the forces of the law.

To highlight the isolation and unfamiliar surroundings, the manuals instruct the police to display an air of confidence in the suspect's guilt and, from outward appearance, to maintain only an interest in confirming certain details. The guilt of the subject is to be posited as a fact. The interrogator should direct his comments toward the reasons why the subject committed the act, rather than court failure by asking the subject whether he did it. Like other men, perhaps the subject has had a bad family life, had an unhappy childhood, had too much to drink, had an unrequited desire for women. The officers are instructed to minimize the moral seriousness of the offense, to cast blame on the victim or on society. These tactics are designed to put the subject in a psychological state where his story is but an elaboration of what the police purport to know already—that he is guilty. Explanations to the contrary are dismissed and discouraged.

The texts thus stress that the major qualities an interrogator should possess are patience and perseverance.

One writer describes the efficacy of these characteristics in this manner:

> In the preceding paragraphs, emphasis has been placed on kindness and stratagems. The investigator will, however, encounter many situations where the sheer weight of his personality will be the deciding factor. Where emotional appeals and tricks are employed to no avail, he must rely on an oppressive atmosphere of dogged persistence. He must interrogate steadily and without relent, leaving the

> subject no prospect of surcease. He must dominate his subject and overwhelm him with his inexorable will to obtain the truth. He should interrogate for a spell of several hours, pausing only for the subject's necessities in acknowledgment of the need to avoid a charge of duress that can be technically substantiated. In a serious case, the interrogation may continue for days, with the required intervals for food and sleep, but with no respite from the atmosphere of domination. It is possible in this way to induce the subject to talk without resorting to duress or coercion. The method should be used only when the guilt of the subject appears highly probable.

The manuals suggest that the suspect be offered legal excuses for his actions in order to obtain an initial admission of guilt. Where there is a suspected revenge killing, for example, the interrogator may say:

> Joe, you probably didn't go out looking for this fellow with the purpose of shooting him. My guess is, however, that you expected something from him, and that's why you carried a gun—for your own protection. You knew him for what he was, no good. Then when you met him, he probably started using foul, abusive language and he gave some indication that he was about to pull a gun on you, and that's when you had to act to save your own life. That's about it, isn't it, Joe?

Having then obtained the admission of shooting, the interrogator is advised to refer to circumstantial evidence which negates the self-defense explanation. This should enable him to secure the entire story. One text notes that,

> Even if he fails to do so, the inconsistency between the subject's original denial of the shooting and his present admission of at least doing the shooting will serve to deprive him of a self-defense 'out' at the time of trial.

When the techniques described above prove unavailing, the texts recommend they be alternated with a show of some hostility. One ploy often used has been termed the "friendly-unfriendly," or the "Mutt and Jeff" act:

> In this technique, two agents are employed. Mutt, the relentless investigator, who knows the subject is guilty and is not going to waste any time. He's sent a dozen men away for this crime, and he's going to send the subject away for the full term. Jeff, on the other hand, is obviously a kindhearted man. He has a family himself. He has a brother who was involved in a little scrape like this. He disapproves of Mutt and his tactics, and will arrange to get him off the case if the subject will cooperate. He can't hold Mutt off for very long. The subject would be wise to make a quick decision. The technique is applied by having both investigators present while Mutt acts out his role. Jeff may stand by quietly and demur at some of Mutt's tactics. When Jeff makes his plea for cooperation, Mutt is not present in the room.

The interrogators sometimes are instructed to induce a confession out of trickery. The technique here is quite effective in crimes which require identification or which run in series. In the identification situation, the interrogator may take a break in his questioning to place the subject among a group of men in a line-up.

> The witness or complainant (previously coached, if necessary) studies the line-up and confidently points out the subject as the guilty party.

Then the questioning resumes "as though there were now no doubt about the guilt of the subject." A variation on this technique is called the "reverse line-up":

> The accused is placed in a line-up, but this time he is identified by several fictitious witnesses or victims who associated him with different offenses. It is expected that the subject will become desperate and confess to the offense under investigation in order to escape from the false accusations.

The manuals also contain instructions for police on how to handle the individual who refuses to discuss the matter entirely, or who asks for an attorney or relatives. The examiner is to concede him the right to remain silent.

> This usually has a very undermining effect. First of all, he is disappointed in his expectation of an unfavorable reaction on the part of the interrogator. Secondly, a concession of this right to remain silent impresses the subject with the apparent fairness of his interrogator.

After this psychological conditioning, however, the officer is told to point out the incriminating significance of the suspect's refusal to talk:

> Joe, you have a right to remain silent. That's your privilege, and I'm the last person in the world who'll try to take it away from you. If that's the way you want to leave this, O. K. But let me ask you this. Suppose you were in my shoes, and I were in yours, and you called me in to ask me about this, and I told you, 'I don't want to answer any of your questions.' You'd think I had something to hide, and you'd probably be right in thinking that. That's exactly what I'll have to think about you, and so will everybody else. So let's sit here and talk this whole thing over.

Few will persist in their initial refusal to talk, it is said, if this monologue is employed correctly.

In the event that the subject wishes to speak to a relative or an attorney, the following advice is tendered:

> The interrogator should respond by suggesting that the subject first tell the truth to the interrogator himself, rather than get anyone else involved in the matter. If the request is for an attorney, the interrogator may suggest that the subject save himself or his family the expense of any such professional service, particularly if he is innocent of the offense under investigation. The interrogator may also add, 'Joe, I'm only looking for the truth, and if you're telling the truth, that's it. You can handle this by yourself.

From these representative samples of interrogation techniques, the setting prescribed by the manuals and observed in practice becomes clear. In essence, it is this: to be alone with the subject is essential to prevent distraction and to deprive him of any outside support. The aura of confidence in his guilt undermines his will to resist. He merely confirms the preconceived story the police seek to have him describe.

> Patience and persistence, at times relentless questioning, are employed. To obtain a confession, the interrogator must "patiently maneuver himself or his quarry into a position from which the desired objective may be attained." When normal procedures fail to produce the needed result, the police may resort to deceptive stratagems such as giving false legal advice. It is important to keep the subject off balance, for example, by trading on his insecurity about himself or his surroundings. The police then persuade, trick, or cajole him out of exercising his constitutional rights.
>
> Even without employing brutality, the "third degree" or the specific stratagems described above, the very fact of custodial interrogation exacts a heavy toll on individual liberty, and trades on the weakness of individuals.[42]

Against this backdrop, the Court reviewed the facts in each of the four companion cases under review and condemned many of the police interrogation techniques in the police manuals the Justices had reviewed:

> It is obvious that such an interrogation environment is created for no purpose other than to subjugate the individual to the will of his examiner. This atmosphere carries its own badge of intimidation. To be sure, this is not physical intimidation, but it is equally destructive of human dignity. The current practice of *incommunicado* interrogation is at odds with one of our Nation's most cherished principles—that the individual may not be compelled to incriminate himself. Unless adequate protective devices are employed to dispel the compulsion inherent in custodial surroundings, no statement obtained from the defendant can truly be the product of his free choice.[43]

The Court also noted that these tactics contributed to false confessions.[44] It therefore established procedural safeguards to protect the privilege against self-incrimination—the familiar ***Miranda* warnings:**

---

42 *Id.* at 449–55 (quoting FRED E. INBAU & JOHN E. REID, CRIMINAL INTERROGATION AND CONFESSIONS (1962); FRED E. INBAU & JOHN E. REID, DETECTION AND CRIMINAL INTERROGATION 185 (3d ed.1953); CHARLES E. O'HARA, FUNDAMENTALS OF CRIMINAL INVESTIGATION (1956) (other internal citations omitted)).

43 *Id.* at 457–58.

44 *Id.* at 445 n.24 (citing, *inter alia*, EDWIN M. BORCHARD, CONVICTING THE INNOCENT (1932); JEROME FRANK & BARBARA FRANK, NOT GUILTY (1957)).

> [W]hen an individual is taken into custody or otherwise deprived of his freedom by the authorities in any significant way and is subjected to questioning, the privilege against self-incrimination is jeopardized. Procedural safeguards must be employed to protect the privilege and unless other fully effective means are adopted to notify the person of his right of silence and to assure that the exercise of the right will be scrupulously honored, the following measures are required. *He must be warned prior to any question that he has the right to remain silent, that anything he says can be used against him in a court of law, that he has the right to the presence of an attorney, and that if he cannot afford an attorney one will be appointed for him prior to any questioning if he so desires.* Opportunity to exercise these rights must be afforded to him throughout the interrogation. After such warnings have been given, and such opportunity afforded him, the individual may knowingly and intelligently waive these rights and agree to answer questions or make a statement. But unless and until such warnings and waiver are demonstrated by the prosecution at trial no evidence obtained as a result of interrogation can be used against him.[45]

No additional warnings are required. Hence, the suspect has no right to be informed of the charges against him or her at the time of arrest or during any custodial interrogation.[46]

A. *Miranda*'s Limitation to Testimonial Evidence

The U.S. Supreme Court has long held that the privilege against self-incrimination applies to **testimonial evidence** and, therefore, does not protect suspects from being compelled to produce real or physical evidence. In other words, the privilege "protects an accused only from being compelled to testify against himself, or otherwise provide the State with evidence of a testimonial or communicative nature. . . ."[47] To be testimonial or communicative, a suspect must "explicitly or implicitly, relate a factual assertion or disclose information. Only then is a person compelled to be a 'witness' against himself."[48] Accordingly, although

---

45 *Id.* at 478–79 (emphasis added).

46 United States v. Clenney, 631 F.3d 658 (4th Cir. 2011).

47 Schmerber v. California, 384 U.S. 757, 761 (1966).

48 Doe v. United States, 487 U.S. 201, 210 (1988).

other constitutional concerns—notably search and seizure and due process ones—might exist when law enforcement officer seeks to have a suspect produce identification or otherwise provide one's name and address, participate in a lineup, provide fingerprints, or give a voice, handwriting, breath, or blood sample because these acts are not testimonial in nature, they raise no Fifth Amendment concerns.

In *Pennsylvania v. Muniz*, police arrested the defendant for driving under the influence and asked him a series of questions without giving him *Miranda* warnings.[49] While responding, his confusion and failure to speak indicated a state of drunkenness. The Court held that *Miranda* did not require suppression of the defendant's responses merely because the slurred nature of his speech was incriminating:

> [Any] evidence of lack of muscular coordination revealed by Muniz's responses to [the officer's] direct questions constitute nontestimonial components of those responses. Requiring a suspect to reveal the physical manner in which he articulates words, like requiring him to reveal the physical properties of the sound produced by his voice . . . does not, without more, compel him to provide a "testimonial" response for purposes of the privilege. [50]

Because *Miranda* warnings are prophylactic measures created to prevent violations of the Fifth Amendment privilege against self-incrimination, *Miranda*'s protections extended only to testimonial evidence. Thus, when law enforcement obtains statements in violation of *Miranda*, only the testimonial evidence—the statements themselves—are subject to suppression at trial from the prosecution's case-in-chief.[51] They may, however, be used to impeach a defendant's testimony at trial.[52] They may even be admissible in the prosecution's case-in-chief if some exigent circumstance, such as an imminent threat to public safety, necessitates the

---

49 Pennsylvania v. Muniz, 496 U.S. 582 (1990).

50 *Id.* at 592 (citing United States v. Dionisio, 410 U.S. 1, 7 (1973) (holding suspects may be compelled to read out-loud to provide voice exemplars because such samples are "used solely to measure the physical properties of the witnesses' voices, not for the testimonial or communicative content of what was to be said")).

51 Chavez v. Martinez, 538 U.S. 760, 790 (2003) ("The exclusion of unwarned statements . . . is a complete and sufficient remedy" for *Miranda* violations).

52 Oregon v. Elstad, 470 U.S. 298 (1993); Harris v. New York, 401 U.S. 222 (1971).

immediate questioning of the defendant.[53] But such exceptions to the use of unwarned statements at trial notwithstanding, because the Self-Incrimination Clause, and hence *Miranda*, are aimed at testimonial evidence exclusively, the U.S. Supreme Court has held that the "fruit of the poisonous tree" doctrine does not apply to *Miranda* violations.[54] Thus, any physical evidence derived from an unwarned but otherwise voluntary confession is not subject to exclusion.[55]

B. The Impact of *Miranda*

Broad cross-sections of the U.S. population decried the *Miranda* decision by expressing the same concerns as the dissenters in the case that its requirements "would severely hamper police officers' ability to investigate cases and protect the public."[56]

> In its immediate aftermath, the *Miranda* opinion was assailed by police, prosecutors, politicians, and media. Police officials complained indignantly that *Miranda* would handcuff their investigative abilities. Politicians linked *Miranda* to rising crime rates: Richard Nixon publicly denounced *Miranda* and other Warren Court decisions as representing a victory of the "crime forces" over the "peace forces" in American society, while individual congressmen called for Chief Justice Earl Warren's impeachment . . . . Newspaper editorials deplored the Warren Court's "coddling of criminals," while cartoonists lampooned the logic of the *Miranda* decision. [57]

Congress disagreed with *Miranda* to such a degree that it attempted to legislatively overrule the case by enacting 18 U.S.C. § 3501, which essentially provided that the admissibility of statements should depend

---

53 New York v. Quarles, 467 U.S. 649, 655–56 (1984) (holding that the defendant's unwarned responses to officers' questions about the location of gun were admissible at trial under the so-called "public safety exception" to *Miranda* because the suspect had been arrested in supermarket while wearing empty shoulder holster).

54 United States v. Patane, 542 U.S. 630, 641–42 (2004).

55 *Id.*

56 Meghan J. Ryan, *Is* Miranda *Good News or Bad News for the Police? The Usefulness of Empirical Evidence*, 50 TEX. TECH L. REV. 81, 82 (2017).

57 Richard A. Leo, *The Impact of* Miranda *Revisited*, 86 J. CRIM. L. & CRIMINOLOGY 621, 622 (1996).

solely on whether they were made voluntarily. In *Dickerson v. United States*, the U.S. Supreme Court struck down that law, reasoning that "*Miranda*, being a constitutional decision of this Court, may not be in effect overruled by an Act of Congress, and we decline to overrule *Miranda* ourselves. We therefore hold that *Miranda* and its progeny in this Court govern the admissibility of statements made during custodial interrogation in both state and federal courts."[58]

Empirical research overwhelmingly suggests that the fears expressed after *Miranda* was decided were overblown, if not completely misplaced. Early studies, most of which were conducted within just a few years after the *Miranda* decision, reported that the case "had only a marginal effect on the ability of the police to successfully elicit admissions and confessions from criminal suspects" and, therefore, had no "significant impact either on the rates of apprehension or conviction of criminal suspects."[59] At least one of these early studies did note a substantial drop of just over 21.5% points in the number of felony suspects who gave statements to Pittsburgh police after the *Miranda* decision, but the authors nonetheless concluded that the decrease did not affect arrest and conviction rates in the city.[60] Another study found that clearance rates via arrest had decreased after *Miranda*, but conviction rates were unchanged.[61] And still another of these studies concluded police had quickly learned to

---

58 Dickerson v. United States, 530 U.S. 428, 432 (2000).

59 Leo, *supra* note 57, at 632 (citing, *inter alia*, John Griffiths & Richard Ayres, Faculty Note, *A Postscript to the* Miranda *Project, Interrogation of Draft Protesters*, 77 YALE L.J. 395 (1967); Richard Medalie, Leonard Zeitz & Paul Alexander, *Custodial Police Interrogation in Our Nation's Capital: The Attempt to Implement* Miranda, 66 MICH. L. REV. 1347 (1968); David W. Neubauer, *Confessions in Prairie City: Some Causes and Effects*, 65 J. CRIM. L. & CRIMINOLOGY 103 (1974); Michael Wald, Richard Ayres, David Hess, Mark Schantz & Charles Whitebread, *Interrogations in New Haven: The Impact of* Miranda, 76 YALE L.J. 1519 (1967); Evelle J. Younger, *Interrogation of Criminal Defendants—Some Views on* Miranda v. Arizona, 35 FORDHAM L. REV. 255 (1966); Evelle J. Younger, *Results of a Survey Conducted in the District Attorney's Office of Los Angeles County Regarding the Effect of the* Miranda *Decision Upon the Prosecution of Felony Cases*, 5 AM. CRIM. L.Q. 32 (1966)).

60 Richard Seeburger & R. Stanton Wettick, Jr., Miranda *in Pittsburgh—A Statistical Study*, 29 U. PITT. L. REV. 1 (1967).

61 NEIL A. MILNER, THE COURT AND LOCAL LAW ENFORCEMENT: THE IMPACT OF *MIRANDA* (1971).

use the *Miranda* warnings to their advantage by showing that statements had been voluntarily obtained even though most of the suspects did not adequately understand their rights.[62]

Notably, these early studies are not only outdated—especially since data for them were primarily gathered within three years of the *Miranda* decision, but also, most of these studies had significant methodological limitations.[63] There have been surprisingly few subsequent studies that have assessed *Miranda*. One of the researchers who engaged in such an endeavor, law professor Paul Cassell, concluded that over the long-term, *Miranda* did, indeed, harm law enforcement by causing the rates of confessions, clearances via arrest, and convictions all to plummet.[64] Cassell's research, however, has been criticized for both its methods and conclusions.[65]

Another researcher who studied the impact of *Miranda* is Dr. Richard Leo, who reported that because more than three-quarters of the suspects in his research sample waived their rights, the requirements of *Miranda* had little overall impact on law enforcement's ability to do its job.[66] Moreover, even in the nearly 25% of cases in which suspects invoked their rights under *Miranda*, there were no statistically significant differences in either charging decision outcomes or conviction rates.[67]

---

62 Lawrence S. Leiken, *Police Interrogation in Colorado: The Implementation of* Miranda, 47 DENV. L.J. 1 (1970).

63 *See* Leo, *supra* note 57, at 646–48.

64 Paul G. Cassell, Miranda*'s Social Costs: An Empirical Reassessment*, 90 NW. U. L. REV. 387, 417 (1996); Paul G. Cassell & Richard Fowles, *Handcuffing the Cops? A Thirty-Year Perspective on Miranda's Harmful Effects on Law Enforcement*, 50 STAN. L. REV. 1055, 1063 (1998) [hereinafter Cassell & Fowles, *Handcuffing the Cops?*]; *see also* Paul G. Cassell & Richard Fowles, *Still Handcuffing the Cops? A Review of Fifty Years of Empirical Evidence of Miranda's Harmful Effects on Law Enforcement*, 97 B.U. L. REV. 685 (2017).

65 *See, e.g.*, John J. Donohue, III, *Did* Miranda *Diminish Police Effectiveness?*, 50 STAN. L. REV. 1147, 1148–49 (1998); Steven J. Schulhofer, *Bashing* Miranda *Is Unjustified—and Harmful*, 20 HARV. J.L. & PUB. POL'Y 347 (1997); Stephen J. Schulhofer, Miranda*'s Practical Effect: Substantial Benefits and Vanishingly Small Social Costs*, 90 NW. U. L. REV. 500, 502 (1996); George C. Thomas III & Richard A. Leo, *The Effects of* Miranda v. Arizona: *"Embedded" in Our National Culture?*, 29 CRIME & JUST. 203, 244 (2002).

66 Leo, *supra* note 57, at 658.

67 *Id.*

Law Professor Meghan J. Ryan noted that Cassell's and Leo's divergent findings on *Miranda*'s impact illustrate the many challenges inherent in conducting empirical studies [that] range from securing reliable data to controlling multiple—often difficult-to-predict—variables."[68] Cassell's research, for instance, started with examining confession rates and later switched to focusing on clearance rates.[69] But there are few reliable data sources for the former because they are not systematically recorded, a limitation that Cassell himself has noted about his data.[70] Clearance rata data are better, largely as a function of the fact that the FBI reports them annually, but still, those data are not always reported accurately by law enforcement agencies who may have different definitions of the term, as well as "changing incentives for showing a higher or lower clearance rate than actually exists."[71] Moreover, like conviction rates, clearance rates are "much more removed from the *Miranda* decision than are confession rates, providing the opportunity for confounding variables—variables that could have contributed to, or even independently caused, any change in observed clearance or conviction rates—to bleed into the analysis."[72]

Given the methodological obstacles to engaging in high-quality quantitative data analyses of *Miranda*'s impact, perhaps qualitative research provides the more salient findings on the matter. Consider that after studying 182 interrogations in three police departments, Richard Leo concluded that *Miranda* had a "civilizing influence on police behavior inside the interrogation room."[73]

> The Warren Court in *Miranda* sent an unmistakable message—to police, to prosecutors, and to trial courts—that strong-arm tactics would no longer be tolerated. In the . . . decades since *Miranda* became law, [U.S.] police interrogation methods have become entirely psychological in nature. To be sure, coercive practices sometimes still occur, but they

---

68 Ryan, *supra* note 56, at 88.

69 *Id.* at 89.

70 Cassell & Fowles, *Handcuffing the Cops?*, *supra* note 64, at 106.

71 Ryan, *supra* note 56, at 91 (citing Donohue, *supra* note 65, at 1151–55).

72 *Id.* at 90.

73 Leo, *supra* note 57, at 668.

> appear to be exceptional. Not surprisingly, however, only rarely are confessions found to be involuntary or suppressed from evidence in trial proceedings due to police improprieties. . . .[74]

Leo also reported that *Miranda* has benefited police by pushing them to become more skilled interrogators.

> *Miranda* has inspired police to develop more specialized, more sophisticated, and seemingly more effective interrogation techniques with which to elicit inculpatory statements from custodial suspects.
>
> * * *
>
> [P]olice have fashioned increasingly subtle and sophisticated interrogation techniques . . . [that] . . . are more psychologically sophisticated than earlier methods. Although the Warren Court may have placed greater restraints on their behavior during custodial questioning, police have met the challenges of *Miranda* by devising increasingly clever and ingenious interrogation strategies with which to persuade suspects to confess.[75]

Perhaps these reasons help to explain that law enforcement officers have not only learned to live with *Miranda*, but also have come "even to love it," especially since waivers largely provide officers with a "safe harbor" for the admission of statements, admission, and confessions from the suspects they interrogate.[76]

---

74 *Id.* at 669.

75 *Id.* at 672, 674.

76 CHARLES FRIED, ORDER AND LAW: ARGUING THE REAGAN REVOLUTION—A FIRSTHAND ACCOUNT 45 (1991); *see also* Sandra Guerra Thompson, *Evading* Miranda: *How* Seibert *and* Patane *Failed To "Save"* Miranda, 40 VAL. U. L. REV. 645, 649 (2006) ("[*Miranda*] insulates a stressful interrogation process from judicial scrutiny to determine whether the confession was voluntarily given [and] in cases in which the rights are invoked, the police may be able to ignore *Miranda*, perhaps deliberately, and elicit statements for impeachment use as well as uncovering other admissible derivative evidence."); *cf.* Susan R. Klein, *Identifying and (Re)Formulating Prophylactic Rules, Safe Harbors, and Incidental Rights in Constitutional Criminal Procedure*, 99 MICH. L. REV. 1030, 1033 (2001) (noting the benefits of a "constitutional safe harbor rule . . . that, if properly followed by the government actor, insulates the government from the argument that the constitutional clause at issue was violated.").

Chapter 5:

Voluntariness and Due Process After *Miranda*

Miranda works in conjunction with the due process voluntariness test. The *Miranda* decision dictates that statements obtained in violation of *Miranda* rights are not admissible even if they were otherwise made voluntarily. And, as the U.S. Supreme Court has said, "the failure to provide *Miranda* warnings in and of itself does not render a confession involuntary."[77] However, although satisfaction of *Miranda*'s requirements is a relevant consideration in determining the voluntariness of a confession, it is not conclusive. Statements given after *Miranda* warnings may nonetheless be inadmissible if they were coerced, rather than voluntary even though such cases "are rare."[78] The following sections explore the various ways in which the due process voluntariness standard might be violated even if the technical requirements of *Miranda* are fully satisfied.

A. Physical Force

Recall that *Brown v. Mississippi* made it clear that police may not use physical force to extract a confession.[79] That is still the law today. Law enforcement officers are authorized to use a reasonable amount of force to

---

77 New York v. Quarles, 467 U.S. 649, 655 n.5 (1984) (recognizing a public safety exception to *Miranda*).

78 Berkemer v. McCarty, 468 U.S. 420, 433 n.20 (1984) (holding that the roadside questioning of a motorist detained pursuant to routine traffic stop did not constitute "custodial interrogation" for purposes of *Miranda*, so that prearrest statements motorist made in answer to such questioning were admissible against the motorist even though he had not been Mirandized prior to being asked if he had consumed any intoxicants).

79 Brown v. Mississippi, 297 U.S. 278 (1936).

make an arrest, defend themselves or others, or stop a fleeing felon. What happens when police lawfully use force, Mirandize someone, and then question the suspect? Consider that experimental research has demonstrated that being tazed even once significantly reduces a person's performance on several measures of cognitive functioning.[80] To date, most courts have rejected claims by defendants that exposure to a conductive energy device (i.e., a taser) rendered them unable to make a knowing and intelligent waiver of their Fifth Amendment rights under *Miranda.*[81]

B. Psychological Coercion by Police and Its Effect on Voluntariness

Tactics that fall shy of physical brutality have proven to be much more difficult to analyze under a due process framework. Coercive conduct by police, including some subtle forms of psychological pressures, might render a resulting statement involuntary and thus violate due process.[82]

As with other facets of constitutional criminal procedure, courts examine the totality of the circumstances to determine if a particular

---

80 Donald M. Dawes, Jeffrey D. Ho, Andrea S. Vincent, Paul C. Nystrom & Brian E. Driver, *The Neurocognitive Effects of a Conducted Electrical Weapon Compared to High Intensity Interval Training and Alcohol Intoxication: Implications for Miranda and Consent*, 53 J. FORENSIC & LEGAL MED. 51, 55 (2018); Donald M. Dawes, Jeffrey D. Ho, Andrea S. Vincent, Paul C. Nystrom, Johanna C. Moore, Lila W. Steinberg, Anne Marie K. Tilton, Michael A. Brave, Marc S. Berris & James R. Miner, *The Neurocognitive Effects of Simulated Use-of-Force Scenarios*, 10 FORENSIC SCI. MED. & PATHOLOGY 9, 16 (2014); Robert J. Kane & Michael D. White, *TASER Exposure and Cognitive Impairment: Implications for Valid* Miranda *Waivers and the Timing of Police Custodial Interrogations*, 15 CRIMINOLOGY & PUB. POL'Y 79, 101 (2015); Michael D. White, Justin T. Ready, Robert J. Kane & Lisa M. Dario, *Examining the Effects of the TASER on Cognitive Functioning: Findings from a Pilot Study with Police Recruits*, 10 J. EXPERIMENTAL CRIMINOLOGY 267 (2014).

81 *See, e.g.*, United States v. Jackson, No. 1:08CR00076SNLJ, 2010 WL 254927, at *1 (E.D. Mo. Jan. 19, 2010); United States v. Patterson, No. 3:09-cr-7(S1)-J-32TEM, 2009 WL 10670083, at *1 (M.D. Fla. June 22, 2009); United States v. Mack, No. 07-238, 2009 WL 580430, at *1 (M.D. La. Mar. 6, 2009); State v. Sudduth, No. 93,633, 2006 WL 90102, at *1 (Kan. Ct. App. Jan. 13, 2006); *cf.* United States v. Chancellor, No. 07-20578-CR, 2008 WL 622937, at *1 (S.D. Fla. Feb. 8, 2008) (holding statement involuntary by relying primarily on factors other than taser exposure).

82 Chavez v. Martinez, 538 U.S. 760, 770–73 (2003) (plurality opinion) (holding that the Fifth Amendment bars the use of involuntary statements at trial).

defendant's statements were involuntary. The test for voluntariness of a statement was stated in *Townsend v. Sain*:

> If an individual's "will was overborne" or if his confession was not "the product of a rational intellect and a free will," his confession is inadmissible because coerced. These standards are applicable whether a confession is the product of physical intimidation or psychological pressure. . . . Any questioning by police officers which, in fact, produces a confession which is not the product of a free intellect renders that confession inadmissible. [83]

The judicial inquiry into voluntariness examines the actions of law enforcement personnel. Police, or people acting at their behest, must create the pressure that overcomes a particular person's will. Without coercion by a state actor, a statement cannot be held involuntary.[84]

Table 1 summarizes the kinds of police conduct that have been held to violate due process.

C. Practices That Do Not Violate Due Process

Merely encouraging a suspect's cooperation in a noncoercive manner, including telling the suspect about the probable penalties, does not violate due process.[85] But sometimes law enforcement does more than merely encourage a suspect to "do the right thing" by promising leniency or psychological treatment, appealing to religious beliefs, confronting the suspect with the evidence against them, and even making misleading or downright false statements. As the following subsections explain, courts routinely find such conduct, without more, usually does not render statements involuntary.

---

83 Townsend v. Sain, 372 U.S. 293, 307–08 (1963).

84 Colorado v. Connelly, 479 U.S. 157, 170 (1986).

85 United States v. Ballard, 586 F.2d 1060 (5th Cir. 1978).

Table 1: Interrogation Tactics That Violate Due Process	
Conduct	*Example(s)*
Threats of violence	• In *Lam v. Kelchner*, the court held a statement to be involuntary because undercover police threatened the defendant with gang violence.[86] • The court excluded the confession in *Griffin v. Strong*, in which a police officer told the suspect that if he did not confess, he would be placed back in the general jail population where jail inmates would "'come down and smash [his] guts all over the floor . . . ."[87]
Other threats	• The court in *People v. Phelps* determined the confession was involuntary because police officers had indicated that a lack of cooperation from a sexual assault suspect would lead to a painful penile swab procedure to obtain evidence.[88] • *State v. Chavarria* invalidated statements as involuntary when they were made after a public employee was threatened with job termination if a statement was not given to police.[89] • Threats to extend a period of incarceration—including through revocation of bail bond, probation, or parole—render a statement involuntary.[90]

86 Lam v. Kelchner, 304 F.3d 256 (3d Cir. 2002).

87 Griffin v. Strong, 983 F.2d 1540, 1543 (10th Cir. 1993).

88 State v. Phelps, 456 N.W.2d 290, 294 (Neb. 1990).

89 State v. Chavarria, 33 P.3d 922, 927 (N.M. Ct. App. 2001).

90 *E.g.*, United States v. Mashburn, 406 F.3d 303, 305 (4th Cir. 2005); State v. Tuttle, 650 N.W.2d 20, 28–29 (S.D. 2002).

Table 1 (continued)	
Conduct	*Example(s)*
Confinement under particularly inhumane conditions	• *Brooks v. Florida* invalidated the confession of a suspect who had been confined naked for thirty-five days in a "windowless sweatbox" that had no furnishings or facilities except for a hole in the floor. During his confinement, he was fed only small amounts of soup and water each day.[91] The court in *United States v. Koch* ruled a confession involuntary because the suspect had been confined in a "boxcar" cell for six hours, during which time he had no visibility outside the cell, no hygiene, and no ability to speak with others.[92]
Interrogation after lengthy, unnecessary delays	• Under 18 U.S.C. § 3501(c), a federal court may exclude a confession when the confession is made after six hours following arrest, but before an initial appearance or arraignment if the delay between arrest and arraignment is unreasonable in light of the means of transportation and the distance traveled to the nearest available magistrate. Several states have adopted similar provisions.[93]
Denial of necessary medical care	• Withholding or threatening not to provide needed medical treatment unless a suspect confesses renders statements made under such conditions involuntary.[94] • Continued interrogation of an injured, depressed, and medicated suspect in extreme pain while being treated in a hospital intensive care unit renders statements involuntary.[95]

91 Brooks v. Florida, 389 U.S. 413 (1967).

92 United States v. Koch, 552 F.2d 1216 (7th Cir. 1977).

93 *E.g.*, Williams v. State, 825 A.2d 1078 (Md. 2003).

94 State v. Wright, 587 N.E.2d 906, 910 (Ohio Ct. App. 1990).

95 Mincey v. Arizona, 437 U.S. 385 (1978).

Table 1 (continued)	
Conduct	*Example(s)*
Deprivations of food or sleep	• Deprivations of food or sleep can result in a confession being found involuntary.[96]
Relay questioning over extended periods	• In *Ashcraft v. Tennessee*, the suspect was interrogated for thirty-six hours with virtually no break, thereby depriving the suspect of any rest. The Court invalidated the confession as involuntary.[97]

1. Promises of Leniency or Psychological Treatment

Promises of leniency in exchange for cooperation with law enforcement officials, whether those promised are express or implied, do not invalidate statements on involuntariness grounds.[98] In *United States v. Kourani*, the defendant made certain admissions to FBI agents "on a condition of confidentiality."[99] Moreover, the agents gave the defendant and his lawyer the impression that the defendant would not face prosecution in exchange for his cooperation. The court determined that, under the totality of the circumstances, the defendant's statements had been made voluntarily, largely because (1) the defendant was intelligent and well-educated; (2) he had previously invoked his right to silence before subsequently agreeing to talk with agents in the presence of his attorney; (3) the agents were dressed in business-casual attire without firearms displayed; and (4) the agent did not coerce the defendant in any way. With regard to the impression that the defendant would be granted immunity, the court said:

> [O]ur precedent dictates "that the presence of a direct or implied promise of help or leniency has not barred the admission of a confession where the totality of the circumstances indicates that it was the product of a free

96 Greenwald v. Wisconsin, 390 U.S. 519 (1968); Watts v. Indiana, 338 U.S. 49 (1949).

97 Ashcraft v. Tennessee, 322 U.S. 143 (1944); *see also* Davis v. North Carolina, 384 U.S. 737 (1966).

98 *See, e.g.*, United States v. Swan, 842 F.3d 28, 34 (1st Cir. 2016) (holding a confession voluntary even though an officer had promised leniency in exchange for the defendant's cooperation); United States v. Guarno, 819 F.2d 28, 31 (2d Cir. 1987) (same).

99 United States v. Kourani, 6 F.4th 345, 352 (2d Cir. 2021).

> and independent decision." Moreover, we cannot hold that the District Court clearly erred when it concluded that the agents did not implicitly adopt [the] memorandum of the meetings [prepared by the defendant's lawyer which] noted that [the defendant] "has committed no crime and faces no prosecution. . . ." The District Court also did not err, much less clearly err, in finding that, in any event, [the defendant and his lawyer] knew or should have known that the FBI agents lacked the authority to promise immunity.[100]

Similarly, promises of certain leniency in sentencing do not render statements involuntary. In *United States v. Higgins-Vogt*, for example,[101] a court ruled the defendant's confession was voluntary even though a government worker, who held herself out as a mental health counselor but was assisting law enforcement, had implied to the defendant that his mental illness would mean he would go to mental institutional rather than prison.[102] Similarly, *United States v. McClinton* upheld a confession as voluntary even though police had told the defendant that "he was not a bad person and that he would receive help for his drug and alcohol problems if he talked to them."[103]

Even though promises of leniency, by themselves, do not render statements involuntary, such promises might be sufficiently coercive when combined with other factors such that statements might be determined to be involuntary. For instance, the defendant in *Rodriguez v. McDonald* was only fourteen years old, had ADHD, and a borderline IQ in the mid-70s.[104] After stating that these factors made him "susceptible to suggestion and coercion," a court found that several police tactics coalesced to overcome the defendant's will, including promises of leniency due to his youthful age.[105] The court noted that even after the defendant requested a lawyer,

> officers continued to pressure him. Though Mr. Rodriguez had repeatedly denied participating in the shooting, the officers told him he

---

[100] *Id.* at 352–53.

[101] United States v. Higgins-Vogt, 911 F.3d 814 (7th Cir. 2018).

[102] *Id.* at 824.

[103] United States v. McClinton, 982 F.2d 278, 283 (8th Cir. 1992).

[104] Rodriguez v. McDonald, 872 F.3d 908 (9th Cir. 2017).

[105] *Id.* at 923.

> would be charged with murder later that day, increasing the urgency of cooperation. An officer reminded Mr. Rodriguez that they had "tried to give [him] the opportunity to straighten things out," recalling the officers' earlier promises of leniency.
>
> This is precisely the type of threat that we have held makes a subsequent reinitiation of interrogation involuntary. . . . By suggesting to Mr. Rodriguez that he would be imminently charged with murder but that cooperation would result in more lenient treatment from the court, the probation office, and from the police themselves, the officers "effectively told Mr. Rodriguez he would be penalized if he exercised rights guaranteed to him under the Constitution of the United States."[106]

Unlike general promises of leniency, however, outright lies about the legal implications of giving a statement typically render that statement involuntary. Thus, *United States v. Lall* ruled a defendant's confession involuntary because an officer "explicitly assured [the defendant] that anything he said would not be used to prosecute him."[107] And in *United States v. Rogers*, a court ruled that an outright promise to suspects that they will not be prosecuted if they confess rendered the defendant's confession involuntary.[108]

2. Appeals to Religious Beliefs

In *Berghuis v. Thompkins*, the U.S. Supreme Court reiterated that "[t]he Fifth Amendment privilege is not concerned 'with moral and psychological pressures to confess emanating from sources other than official coercion.'"[109] Accordingly, the Court ruled that a detective's question about whether the defendant "prayed to God for forgiveness for shooting the victim" merely referred to religious beliefs and, as such, did

---

[106] *Id.* at 924 (internal alterations omitted) (quoting Collazo v. Estelle, 940 F.2d 411, 413–14 (9th Cir. 1991) (en banc)).

[107] United States v. Lall, 607 F.3d 1277, 1287 (11th Cir. 2010).

[108] United States v. Rogers, 906 F.2d 189, 191 (5th Cir. 1990); *see also* Albritton v. State, 769 So. 2d 438, 442 (Fla. Dist. Ct. App. 2000).

[109] Berghuis v. Thompkins, 560 U.S. 370, 387 (2010) (internal alterations omitted) (quoting Colorado v. Connelly, 479 U.S. 157, 170 (1986)).

not render the defendant's subsequent incriminating statements involuntary.[110]

This particular facet of the decision in *Berghuis v. Thompkins* reveals no new Fifth Amendment jurisprudence. Consider that more than twenty years earlier, in *Welch v. Butler*, a born-again Christian police officer had orchestrated and led a nearly three-hour prayer session with the suspect, during which he used his religious beliefs concerning divine forgiveness and salvation to convince the suspect to confess.[111] In upholding the voluntariness of the defendant's confession, a federal appeals court stated

> Although religious speculation about the "voluntariness" of yielding to the will of God or of submitting to teaching that advocates so yielding has its place, it is not relevant to the issue before us. . . . One does not have to be devout to accept the fact that Welch was concerned about his salvation and about divine forgiveness. However, this concern existed before his conversations with [the officer]. At most, the police set up a situation that allowed Welch to focus for some time on those concerns with a fellow Christian in the hope that his desire to be saved would lead him to confess.[112]

3. Confronting the Defendant with Evidence of Guilt

Law enforcement officers may confront suspects with the evidence of guilt that they amass during an investigation. When faced with such evidence, many suspects break down and confess. But such a reaction does not render their confessions involuntary.[113] That holds true even when officers show photos of victims that might play on a suspect's emotions.[114]

In *United States v. Sablotny*, a detective questioned a sixty-two-year-old woman about her role in the arson of a bar she owned.[115] During the interrogation, the detective confronted the suspect with the fact that a part-

---

[110] *Id.*

[111] Welch v. Butler, 835 F.2d 92 (5th Cir. 1988).

[112] *Id.* at 95.

[113] *See, e.g.*, United States v. Morgan, 738 F.3d 1002, 1005–06 (9th Cir. 2013); United States v. Byers, 649 F.3d 197, 216 (4th Cir. 2011); United States v. Guarno, 819 F.2d 28, 31 (2d Cir. 1987).

[114] *See, e.g.*, United States v. Sanchez, 614 F.3d 876, 885–86 (8th Cir. 2010).

[115] United States v. Sablotny, 21 F.3d 747 (7th Cir. 1994).

time bartender at the establishment had already confessed that he had set the fire at her request.[116] He also told her that she would likely go to jail. She eventually confessed but sought to have her confession set aside as involuntary on the grounds that, in combination with her age, the detective's repeated questioning of her—which included him repeating her accomplice's accusations and mentioning the likelihood of a jail sentence—had overcome her will. Both a trial and appeals court rejected her claims, with the latter reasoning as follows:

> Ms. Sablotny argues that Mitchell kept repeating questions and reiterating Yucas' accusations. She contends that this procedure was coercive. However, "an interrogating officer's act of merely informing the accused of the nature of the evidence implicating him, without more, does not constitute coercive police conduct." Ms. Sablotny testified that Mitchell told her that she would probably go to jail. She argues that this was coercive. *But the police are allowed to play on a suspect's ignorance, fears, and anxieties so long as they do not magnify these emotionally charged matters to the point where a rational decision becomes impossible.* Under this standard, the police did not exceed their bounds by frightening Ms. Sablotny with the specter of jail, a prospect of which she must have been well aware in any event.[117]

4. Trickery and Deception by Police and Their Effect on Voluntariness

"Deceit and subterfuge are within the 'bag of tricks' that police may use in interrogating suspects."[118] The U.S. Supreme Court and the high courts of virtually all U.S. states have all decided cases that collectively permit police in the United States to lie to suspects during

---

[116] *Id.* at 749–50.

[117] *Id.* at 752–53 (italics added) (quoting Ray v. Duckworth, 881 F.2d 512, 518 (7th Cir. 1989), and citing United States v. Rutledge, 900 F.2d 1127, 1130 (7th Cir.), *cert. denied*, 498 U.S. 875 (1990)).

[118] State v. Schumacher, 37 P.3d 6, 13–14 (Idaho Ct. App. 2001).

interrogations.[119] *Frazier v. Cupp* is one of the most well-known cases to so hold.[120]

In *Frazier*, the police obtained a confession from a defendant after lying to him that his accomplice had already confessed to the crime. After noting that the defendant was an adult of ordinary intelligence and that the questioning was of "short duration, the U.S. Supreme Court said, "[t]he fact that the police misrepresented the statements that [the accomplice] had made is, while relevant, insufficient in our view to make this otherwise voluntary confession inadmissible."[121] It therefore upheld the voluntariness of the confession.

The facts in *Frazier* are quite common. As one commentator said,

> [I]t is rather stunning to see the enormous number of cases in which confessions were held to be valid. Yet, judges found that government officials lied to defendants about significant matters resulting in incriminating statements. Police have lied about matters such as the following: witnesses against the defendant, earlier statements by a now-deceased victim, an accomplice's willingness to testify, whether the victim had survived an assault, "scientific" evidence available, including DNA and fingerprint evidence, and the degree to which the investigating officer identified and sympathized with the defendant.
>
> For the Supreme Court Justices and judges throughout the nation, no matter the nature of the deception, with [few] major exceptions, the issue relates entirely to whether the lies "tend to produce inherently unreliable statements." Or, as another court stated, whether the "police misrepresentations . . . [are] sufficiently egregious to overcome a defendant's will so as to render a confession involuntary."[122]

In spite of the general proposition that police may use trickery or deceit during interviews and interrogations, some ruses can go too far. Courts are particularly suspicious of three types of deceptions.

---

[119] Paul Marcus, *It's Not Just About* Miranda*: Determining the Voluntariness of Confessions in Criminal Prosecutions*, 40 VAL. U. L. REV. 601, 612 (2006); *see also* Frazier v. Cupp, 394 U.S. 731 (1969).

[120] *Frazier*, 394 U.S. at 739.

[121] *Id.*

[122] Marcus, *supra* note 119, at 612–13 (internal citations omitted).

First, false threats are the quintessential type of behavior that renders statements involuntary. Recall, for example, *Lam v. Kelchner*, which was briefly summarized in Table 1.[123] The court in that case determined the defendant's confession was involuntary because police had represented themselves as gang members and threatened the fearful defendant with physical harm.[124] But as previously discussed, threats of physical harm are not the only types of threats that can invalidate a statement from a suspect, including "potential prosecution or arrest of friends and family; greater terms of incarceration; lack of protection against others who threaten the suspect; use, or refusal to authorize use, of medical treatment; loss of employment or education; and forfeiture of drivers' licenses."[125]

Second, misrepresentations about the legal process can be a decisive factor in rendering a statement involuntary. For instance, courts often invalidate statements suspects make after police lie to the suspects that they will be released if they confess, or that they will not be prosecuted.[126]

Courts are similarly hostile to false claims about the nature of interrogation. Thus, for instance, *United States v. Giddins* held the defendant's confession involuntary because when police misled him by telling him that he was "required to submit to questioning in order to have his vehicle returned to him."[127] Moreover, they told him was not "in

---

[123] Lam v. Kelchner, 304 F.3d 256 (3d Cir. 2002).

[124] *Id.* at 264–67.

[125] Marcus, *supra* note 119, at 619–20 (citing, *inter alia*, United States v. Mashburn, 406 F.3d 303, 305 (4th Cir. 2005); State v. Tuttle, 650 N.W.2d 20, 28–29 (S.D. 2002); State v. Bowe, 881 P.2d 538, 547 (Haw. 1994); People v. Thomas, 839 P.2d 1174, 1178 (Colo. 1992); Black v. State, 820 P.2d 969, 972 (Wyo. 1991); State v. Pilcher, 472 N.W.2d 327, 334 (Minn. 1991); People v. McIntyre, 789 P.2d 1108, 1110 (Colo. 1990); State v11111. Phelps, 456 N.W.2d 290, 294 (Neb. 1990); Webb v. State, 756 P.2d 293, 296 (Alaska 1988); State v. Chavarria, 33 P.3d 922, 927 (N.M. Ct. App. 2001); State v. Baker, 521 S.E.2d 24, 26 (Ga. Ct. App. 1999); State v. Strayhand, 911 P.2d 577, 585 (Ariz. Ct. App. 1995); State v. Corns, 426 S.E.2d 324, 327 (S.C. Ct. App. 1992); State v. Wright, 587 N.E.2d 906, 910 (Ohio Ct. App. 1990); People v. Keene, 539 N.Y.S.2d 214 (App. Div. 1989); State v. Foster, 729 P.2d 599, 604 (Or. Ct. App. 1986)).

[126] Marcus, *supra* note 119, at 616–17 (citing, *inter alia*, Albritton v. State, 769 So. 2d 438, 442 (Fla. Dist. Ct. App. 2000); Johnson v. State, 721 So. 2d 650, 659 (Miss. Ct. App. 1998); Smith v. State, 787 P.2d 1038, 1039 (Alaska Ct. App. 1990); State v. Edwards, 338 S.E.2d 126, 127 (N.C. Ct. App. 1985)).

[127] United States v. Giddins, 858 F.3d 870, 885 (4th Cir. 2017).

trouble" even though they had secured a warrant to arrest him.[128] *Hopkins v. Cockrell* similarly ruled a confession involuntary when a detective misled the defendant to believe that their conversation was confidential.[129]

And lies about the severity of the crime can also render a confession involuntary. In *State v. Ritter*, for instance, the police lied to induce a suspect into making a statement that incriminated himself by telling him that the victim of an assault was alive, when, in fact, the victim was deceased.[130] The court reasoned as follows:

> [The detective's] representation regarding the victim's state of health constituted an implied promise that Ritter could not be charged with murder if he gave a statement to the police, but could only be charged with aggravated assault on a victim who was represented to be not only still alive but actively recovering and suffering from nothing more than a bad headache. Given [the detective's] testimony that the representations were made to induce Ritter to speak based on the detective's assessment that Ritter would invoke his right to remain silent if he knew the full extent of the charges against him, the evidence supports the conclusion that Ritter was induced to talk to the police under the belief that he was incriminating himself only in regard to an aggravated assault charge and thus his confession was based upon the hope that he faced a lighter possible criminal penalty than he actually was facing.[131]

Third, although fabrications concerning the evidence against a suspect might not, in and of themselves, render a statement involuntary, courts have viewed the manufacture of false evidence by law enforcement officials to incriminate the suspect as having crossed an impermissible line for due process purposes. *State v. Patton*, for example, ruled a confession involuntary when the suspect was presented with an audiotape of an

---

128 *Id.*

129 Hopkins v. Cockrell, 325 F.3d 579, 584–85 (5th Cir. 2003); *see also* United States v. Lall, 607 F.3d 1277, 1287 (11th Cir. 2010) (holding a confession involuntary because an officer assured the defendant that anything said would not be used against defendant).

130 State v. Ritter, 485 S.E.2d 492 (Ga. 1997).

131 *Id.* at 495.

alleged eyewitness when the voice was actually that of a police officer.[132] And *State v. Cayward* invalidated a confession made after police presented the suspect with a fake lab report matching the suspect's DNA to crime scene evidence.[133]

D. The Effect of Particular Personal Characteristics of Suspects on Voluntariness

As the descriptions of some cases discussed thus far indicate, courts also examine the personal characteristics of defendants in determining the voluntariness of an admission or confession. Some of the characteristics considered important are age; mental capacity; education level; physical or mental impairment from illness, injury, or intoxication; and experience in dealing with the police. However, the U.S. Supreme Court emphasized that any of these personal characteristics are "relevant only in establishing a setting in which actual coercion might have been exerted to overcome the will of the suspect."[134] This principle was elaborated upon in *Colorado v. Connelly.*[135]

> [W]hile mental condition is surely relevant to an individual's susceptibility to police coercion, mere examination of the confessant's state of mind can never conclude the due process inquiry. . . . *[C]oercive police activity is a necessary predicate to the finding that a confession is not "voluntary"* within the meaning of the Due Process Clause of the Fourteenth Amendment.[136]

Of course, states may provide more protection than the U.S. Constitution does with respect to determining the voluntariness of a confession or the validity of a *Miranda* waiver. At least two states, Maine and Hawaii, have expressly rejected the notion that state action is a necessary prerequisite to finding a statement involuntary and, therefore, violative of state constitutional due process guarantees.

---

[132] State v. Patton, 826 A.2d 783 (N.J. Super. App. Div. 2003).

[133] State v. Cayward, 552 So. 2d 971 (Fla. Dist. Ct. App. 1989).

[134] Procunier v. Atchley, 400 U.S. 446, 453–54 (1971).

[135] Colorado v. Connelly, 479 U.S. 157 (1986).

[136] *Id.* at 165–67 (emphasis added).

In *State v. Rees*, the Maine Supreme Court found that because the defendant suffered from dementia, his statements to police officers were not the product of the free exercise of his will and rational intellect.[137] The court stressed that there was no finding of improper or incorrect conduct on the part of the police.[138] The decision pointed out that the determination that the defendant's dementia rendered him incapable of making a voluntary statement under the circumstances was based not on the Fifth or Fourteenth Amendments to the U.S. Constitution, but rather on the Maine Constitution.

And in *State v. Bowe*, the Supreme Court of Hawaii stated the following:

> [T]he absence of police coercion does not foreclose a finding of involuntariness. Rather, we recognize . . . that the issue of voluntariness must be resolved by evaluating the "totality of circumstances" surrounding the making of the statement regardless of whether the source of the coercion was a private individual or the state.[139]

The court then found a suspect's statements to be involuntary because he felt compelled to make them as a result of his basketball coach telling him that he had to go to a police station and have a conversation with a particular detective. The defendant "believed that he could not refuse to follow [his coach's] directions because if he did so, [the coach] could suspend him from the Basketball Team or institute procedures to revoke [the defendant's] athletic scholarship."[140]

Although an appellate court in Illinois declined to depart from *Connelly*'s holding with regard to state action, the court did part ways with *Connelly*'s logic concerning the validity of waivers, reasoning that individual characteristics such as mental illness or substandard intelligence can deprive someone of making a knowing waiver of *Miranda*

---

137 State v. Rees, 748 A.2d 976 (Me. 2000).

138 *Id.* at 977.

139 State v. Bowe, 881 P.2d 538, 547 (1994).

140 *Id.*

rights, even in the absence of any state action calling into question the voluntariness of such a waiver.[141]

> In the instant case, the [trial] court found, based on its observations of the defendant, that the defendant had substantial difficulty in understanding relatively routine questions, and that the defendant was not only limited in his comprehension of single words, but was substantially unable to understand relatively simple concepts. The court also found that the defendant's confession was the product of his sub-normal intelligence, his inability to comprehend what his rights were, and his fright of the situation. Furthermore, the court stated that it was convinced from the testimony of the psychologist that the defendant would have agreed to and signed most anything placed in front of him during the interrogation process. We believe that the trial court's findings . . . are sufficient to conclude that the defendant did not knowingly waive his *Miranda* rights.[142]

---

141 People v. Bernasco, 541 N.E.2d 774, 782 (Ill. App. Ct. 1989), *aff'd*, 562 N.E.2d 958 (Ill. 1990).

142 *Id.*

Chapter 6:

When Does *Miranda* Apply?

Miranda requires that specific warnings be given to suspects subject to custodial interrogation, regardless of whether the police are investigating a felony or a misdemeanor. The Supreme Court defined the term **custodial interrogation** as "questioning initiated by law enforcement officers after a person has been taken into custody or otherwise deprived of his freedom of action in any significant way."[143] Although the rule seems straightforward enough, several issues arise in cases regarding the application of *Miranda* that typically hinge on the meaning of four terms: *custody*, *interrogation*, *warning*, and *waiver*. Before exploring the meanings of each of these terms, it should be emphasized that *Miranda* warnings technically do not need to be given until custodial interrogation begins. Police are well advised, however, to provide all suspects with their *Miranda* warnings upon taking them into custody, even if they do not intend to question a suspect right away. This may help to ensure that any custodial statement will be admissible in court.

A. Custody

The U.S. Supreme Court has not been consistent in its definition of *custody* for *Miranda* purposes. Lower courts often examine **custody** in response to this question: would a reasonable person in the suspect's position have felt free "to terminate the interrogation and leave"?[144] But the "free to leave" test has been called into question by other U.S. Supreme Court decisions that focus instead on the indicia of arrest. To be clear, a

---

143 Miranda v Arizona, 384 U.S. 436, 444 (1966).

144 Thompson v. Keohane, 516 U.S. 99, 112 (1995), *superseded on other grounds by statute*, 28 U.S.C. § 2254(d).

formal arrest is not necessary. Rather, a person is considered *in custody* if there has been a deprivation of "freedom of action . . . in any significant way,"[145]

Regardless of the somewhat inconsistent ways in which the question of custody is phrased, courts consider the totality of the circumstances surrounding the questioning of a suspect using an objective test that considers the viewpoint of a reasonable person who is "neither guilty of criminal conduct and thus overly apprehensive nor insensitive to the seriousness of the circumstances.[146]

The circumstances that are typically evaluated when trying to determine whether a suspect was in custody include the following criteria:

- the degree of restraint or force used to physically detain the suspect;
- the location of the encounter and whether it was familiar to the suspect or at least neutral or public;
- the number of officers questioning the suspect;
- the duration and character of the interrogation, including the degree of psychological coercion used to detain the individual;
- the language used to summon the suspect;
- the extent to which the suspect is confronted with evidence of guilt; and
- whether the suspect initiated contact with the police.

Other factors may be relevant in any particular case, and no one particular factor is determinative of the issue. Some factors, however, that may be relevant for determining the voluntariness of a confession may not be relevant to determinations of whether someone is in custody for *Miranda* purposes. For example, in *Yarborough v. Alvarado*,[147] the U.S. Supreme Court held that courts should not consider a person's experience with the police when examining the question of custody. The lower court

---

145 Howes v. Fields, 565 U.S. 499, 518 (2012) (Ginsburg, J., concurring) (quoting *Miranda*, 384 U.S. at 467).

146 United States v. Bengivenga, 845 F.2d 593, 596 (5th Cir. 1988).

147 Yarborough v. Alvarado, 541 U.S. 652 (2004).

in the case had suppressed a confession given by a seventeen-year-old defendant. It reasoned that a juvenile is more likely to feel he is not free to leave a police station during questioning than an adult would be. But in reversing the lower court, the Court determined that requiring police to consider the individual characteristics of a suspect when determining the issue of custody would transform what is supposed to be an objective test into a subjective one that would be more difficult for officers to understand and apply to the facts of any given case. Thus, the inquiry is confined to the "objective circumstances of the interrogation."[148]

1. Age

Prior to *Alvarado*, nearly all jurisdictions that had addressed the issue of whether juvenile status may be relevant to the *Miranda* custody determination held that juvenile status was a proper consideration.[149] After *Alvarado*, some state and federal courts continued to consider age, either as a factor in the "totality of the circumstances" review or by analyzing whether a "reasonable juvenile" would have felt free to terminate the interview.[150] Other courts concluded that *Alvarado* prohibited consideration of a juvenile suspect's age in a *Miranda* custody analysis.[151] This disagreement prompted the U.S. Supreme Court to decide *J.D.B. v. North Carolina*.[152]

On the afternoon of September 29, 2005, a uniformed police officer removed J.D.B., a thirteen-year-old, special-education student, from his seventh-grade social studies class.[153] He was escorted to a conference room in his middle school where three adults—two school officials and another police officer—were waiting. The door to the conference room was then closed, and police questioned J.D.B. for between thirty and forty-

---

148 *Id.* at 669 (quoting Stansbury v. California, 511 U.S. 318, 323 (1994)).

149 *E.g.*, A.M. v. Butler, 360 F.3d 787 (7th Cir. 2004); People v. Braggs, 810 N.E.2d 472 (Ill. 2004).

150 *See* Murray v. Earle, 405 F.3d 278 (5th Cir. 2005); *In re* C.H., 763 N.W.2d 708 (Neb. 2009).

151 *E.g.*, *In re* J.F. 987 A.2d 1168 (D.C. 2010); *In re* C.S.C., 118 P.3d 970 (Wyo. 2005).

152 J.D.B. v. North Carolina, 564 U.S. 261 (2011).

153 *Id.* at 265.

five minutes about some neighborhood break-ins in which he was a suspect.[154]

The officers who interrogated J.D.B. never told him that he had the right to remain silent, that he was free to leave at any time, or that he could have a family member present during questioning.[155] At one point, the assistant principal told J.D.B. that he should "do the right thing because the truth always comes out in the end."[156] J.D.B. then incriminated himself when he asked whether he would "still be in trouble" if he returned the stolen items.[157] One of the police officers replied that "it would be helpful," but that "this thing is going to court . . . what's done is done."[158] The officer then told J.D.B. that if he was going to continue breaking into people's houses, he "would have to look at getting a secure custody order" that would result in J.D.B. being "sent to juvenile detention before court."[159] Only at that point did the officer tell J.D.B. that he did not have to talk to him and that he could leave if he wanted to.[160] "Asked whether he understood, J.D.B. nodded and provided further detail, including information about the location of the stolen items. Eventually, J.D.B. wrote a statement" containing the relevant details.[161] He was then permitted to ride the school bus home.

The state filed two juvenile petitions against J.D.B., alleging counts of breaking and entering, as well as larceny.[162] His public defender unsuccessfully sought to have J.D.B.'s statements and the evidence derived from them suppressed because (1) they were obtained in violation of *Miranda*, and (2) they were made involuntarily.[163] After two state appellate courts upheld the adjudication of delinquency, the U.S. Supreme Court reversed, ruling that a minor's age properly informs *Miranda*'s

---

[154] *Id.*

[155] *Id.* at 266.

[156] *Id.*

[157] *Id.*

[158] *Id.*

[159] *Id.* at 266–67.

[160] *Id.* at 267.

[161] *Id.*

[162] *Id.*

[163] *Id.* at 267–68.

custody analysis under the totality of the circumstances because children's ability to withstand coercion markedly differs from those of adults.[164] The Court explained:

> So long as the child's age was known to the officer at the time of the interview, or would have been objectively apparent to any reasonable officer, including age as part of the custody analysis requires officers neither to consider circumstances "unknowable" to them . . . , nor to "anticipate the frailties or idiosyncrasies" of the particular suspect whom they question. . . . The same "wide basis of community experience" that makes it possible, as an objective matter, "to determine what is to be expected" of children in other contexts . . . likewise makes it possible to know what to expect of children subjected to police questioning.
>
> * * *
>
> This is not to say that a child's age will be a determinative, or even a significant, factor in every case. . . . It is, however, a reality that courts cannot simply ignore.[165]

The following sections explore in more detail the other objective criteria that courts use to make this determination under the totality of the circumstances.

2. The Degree of Physical Restraint or Force Used to Physically Detain a Suspect

An absence of physical restraint and the lack of any use of force indicates a noncustodial interrogation.[166] Conversely, curtailing a person's freedom of movement in a manner or to a degree that constitutes the functional equivalent of arrest indicates custody.[167] The clearest example of such a functional equivalent of arrest is the physical restraint of the suspect, such as handcuffing. In *United States v. Bailey*, for instance, the officer told the defendant that he "was not under arrest, but only being detained while a search was conducted."[168] But because the officer

---

164 *Id.* 271–72.

165 *Id.* 274, 277.

166 United States v. Plumman, 409 F.3d 919 (8th Cir. 2005).

167 Stansbury v. California, 511 U.S. 318, 325 (1994).

168 United States v. Bailey, 743 F.3d 322 (2d Cir. 2014).

handcuffed the defendant, the court found he was in custody, reasoning that a reasonable person associates handcuffing with formal arrest.[169]

Of course, a person can be restrained without being in handcuffs. If, for example, an officer holds a gun on a suspect, the officer creates a custodial situation.[170] But even without the use of handcuffs or weapons, suspects can be in custody for *Miranda* purposes if their ability to leave is physically cut off by law enforcement. For example, in *United States v. Giddins*, the court determined that the defendant was in custody even though he had voluntarily gone to a police station and was being told that he was free to leave.[171] Despite such facts that typically are indicia of a noncustodial encounter, the physical setting outweighed such criteria.

> It is true that one door was unlocked in the interrogation room, but it was the door past the questioning detective. The door immediately behind [the defendant] was locked, so in order to leave the room, [he] would have had to walk past [a detective]. Additionally, at least twice during the interrogation, Det. Taylor moved [the defendant's] Giddins's phone away from [him] . . . . Finally . . . , [the defendant] was not able to leave the interrogation room because he believed that if he terminated the interview, he would not have his car returned to him.[172]

Not all physical restraints of a suspect, however, will give rise to a finding of custody. For instance, if someone other than a law enforcement officer restrains a person, the restraint does not constitute custody for *Miranda* purposes. Thus, the court in *Wilson v. Coon* determined that the defendant was not in custody even though an emergency medical technician had briefly restrained the defendant for medical purposes after an accident.[173]

---

[169] *Id.* at 340–41.

[170] *See, e.g.*, Rivera v. Thompson, 879 F.3d 7, 14–15 (1st Cir. 2018) (finding custody because an officer stopped the defendant at gunpoint and questioned him about a stabbing that had occurred close to the location of the stop).

[171] United States v. Giddins, 858 F.3d 870, 880 (4th Cir. 2017).

[172] *Id.* at 880.

[173] Wilson v. Coon, 808 F.2d 688 (8th Cir. 1987).

3. The Location of the Encounter

The place of interrogation is an important but not necessarily conclusive factor in determining custody for *Miranda* purposes. As a rule, interrogation in public places such as stores, restaurants, bars, streets, and sidewalks is usually considered noncustodial because people are in such locations by personal choice, are not isolated from the outside world, and rarely present a police-dominated atmosphere. Table 2 summarizes the indicia of custody at common nonpublic locations.

Table 2: The Role of Location in Determining Custody		
Location	*Indicia of Custodial Finding*	*Indicia of Noncustodial Finding*
Police stations	Stationhouse questioning of suspects is the most police-dominated of environments and thus is one of the most inherently intimidating atmospheres in which someone may be questioned by police.[174]	If suspects voluntarily agree to go to a police station for questioning, that is a strong indicator of a noncustodial encounter.[175] Even if the police transport a suspect to a stationhouse, if suspects volunteer to go with police after being told they are not under arrest, then the questioning is likely to be considered noncustodial,[176] unless other indicia of custody subsequently materialize.[177]
Crime scenes	*Miranda* specifically stated that "general on-the-scene questioning as to facts surrounding a crime or other general questioning of citizens in the fact-finding process" is not an indicator of custody.[178]	When someone is restrained at a crime scene to a degree associated with formal arrest—such as when a suspect is handcuffed—such restraint indicates custody for *Miranda* purposes.[179]

174 *See, e.g.*, Parsad v. Greiner, 337 F.3d 175, 182 (2d Cir. 2003) (holding the defendant was in custody despite having voluntarily gone to the police station because, once there, officers seized his pants during questioning).

175 *See, e.g.*, Peoples v. Campbell, 377 F.3d 1208, 1228 (11th Cir. 2004).

176 *See, e.g.*, Mason v. Mitchell, 320 F.3d 604 (6th Cir. 2003); *see also* United States v. Swan, 842 F.3d 28, 31–33 (1st Cir. 2016).

177 *See, e.g.*, United States v. Slaight, 620 F.3d 816, 819–20, 822 (7th Cir. 2010) (finding the suspect was in custody despite the fact that he voluntarily went to the police station and was told he was free to leave, largely because he was questioned in tiny room for an hour, free egress from which was difficult given three persons being in small room, and he knew that officers had enough evidence to arrest him).

178 Miranda v. Arizona, 384 U.S. 436, 477 (1966).

179 United States v. Horton, 490 F. Supp. 2d 1161 (D. Kan. 2007).

Table 2 (continued)		
Location	*Indicia of Custodial Finding*	*Indicia of Custodial Finding*
Prisons and jails	Incarceration alone is insufficient to constitute custody for *Miranda* purposes.[180] Custody in this context depends on a change in the surroundings of a prisoner, which results in an added imposition on his freedom of movement such as being handcuffed, shackled, or escorted to a location from which the inmate is not permitted to leave.[181]	An inmate was not "in custody" for *Miranda* purposes during an interview in a prison library because he was told that he did not have to answer questions, was not restrained, and was free to leave the library at any time.[182]
Hospitals	When a suspect is brought to the hospital by police and is not "free to leave" because the suspect is handcuffed, then such hospital-based detention is likely to be held to be custodial for *Miranda* purposes.[183]	Custody is not established because a suspect is unable to leave the hospital due to his or her medical condition. A hospital setting lacks a compelling atmosphere, questioning is routine, and the suspect, although confined, is not confined by the police.[184]

[180] Howes v. Fields, 565 U.S. 499, 515–17 (2012); Maryland v. Shatzer, 559 U.S. 98, 113 (2010).

[181] *See, e.g.*, United States v. Cheely, 36 F.3d 1439, 1447 (9th Cir. 1994); United States v. Chamberlain, 163 F.3d 499, 503–04 (8th Cir. 1998).

[182] *See, e.g.*, United States v. Ellison, 632 F.3d 727, 730 (1st Cir. 2010); *see also* United States v. Menzer, 29 F.3d 1223 (7th Cir. 1994).

[183] *See, e.g.*, State v. Lescard, 517 A.2d 1158 (N.H. 1986).

[184] *See, e.g.*, State v. Pontbriand, 878 A.2d 227 (Vt. 2005); People v. Milhollin, 751 P.2d 43, 50 (Colo.1988).

Table 2 (continued)		
Location	*Indicia of Custodial Finding*	*Indicia of Custodial Finding*
Homes	When suspects' freedom of movement in their homes has been significantly restrained, then questioning suspects at home may become custodial. For example, *United States v. Madoch* determined a suspect was in custody because agents rushed into the home; ordered the suspect into the kitchen; and told her not to leave the room, answer the phone, or attend to her six-month-old baby without being escorted by an agent.[185] Custody may similarly be found if suspects are subjected to other indicia of arrest at home, like being handcuffed or having weapons targeted at them.[186]	Ordinarily, interrogation of a person in his or her home is noncustodial because the person is in familiar surroundings and there is no police-dominated atmosphere.[187] However, if police turn a home into a police-dominated environment, an interrogation might be deemed custodial. For example, *United States v. Mittel-Carey* found custody in the home because eight officers maintained physical control over the defendant and interrogated him for 90 to 120 minutes, starting at 6:25 A.M.[188]

185 United States v. Madoch, 149 F.3d 596 (7th Cir. 1998).

186 *See, e.g.*, United States v. Hashime, 734 F.3d 278, 283–85 (4th Cir. 2013) (finding custody because the suspect was awakened at gunpoint, isolated while questioned for three hours in a basement storage room, and told had he had to remain under guard); United States v. Cavazos, 668 F.3d 190, 194–95 (5th Cir. 2012) (finding custody at home the defendant was initially handcuffed, isolated from family, and monitored when using the phone and the restroom).

187 *See* Beckwith v. United States, 425 U.S. 341, 342, 345–47 (1976); United States v. Melo, 954 F.3d 334, 343 (1st Cir. 2020) (finding no custody even though agents questioned the defendant for three hours because it occurred at home, the defendant was allowed to leave his kitchen and remained able to interact with his wife).

188 United States v. Mittel-Carey, 493 F.3d 36, 39–40 (1st Cir. 2007); *see also* Orozco v. Texas, 394 U.S. 324, 325–26 (1969) (finding the suspect was in custody in his home because several officers interrogated him at 4:00 A.M.).

Table 2 (continued)		
Location	*Indicia of Custodial Finding*	*Indicia of Custodial Finding*
Places of business	As with homes, when someone's freedom of movement at work has been significantly restrained, such as when placed in a closely confined area and confronted by police, then questioning a suspect at work may become custodial.[189]	Absent indicia of arrest that can transform questioning in the workplace into a custodial setting for *Miranda* purposes, interrogation at a suspect's place of business is usually noncustodial because it represents familiar surroundings.[190]

4. The Number of Officers Questioning the Suspect

The more police officers present at the scene of questioning, the more complete the police control is over the interrogation environment, a factor indicating that a suspect was in custody. *Sprosty v. Buchler*, for example, determined a suspect was in custody for *Miranda* purposes because five officers dominated the scene in which he was questioned.[191] The entire encounter lasted for nearly three hours, during which four officers searched the defendant's mobile home, and a fifth "armed officer was exclusively occupied with guarding" the defendant.[192] However, the number of officers is only one of many factors considered when applying the totality-of-the-circumstances test for custody. For instance, the same number of officers questioning a suspect in *United States v. Quinn* was determined to be noncustodial, largely because the questioning lasted for only twenty-five minutes and occurred outside on the suspect's driveway.[193] And *United States v. Wright*, the presence of between seventeen and nineteen officers, while "startling and intimidating," was nonetheless determined to be noncustodial because the interrogation took

189 United States v. Steele, 648 F. Supp. 1375 (N.D. Ind. 1986).

190 United States v. Elliott, 876 F.3d 855, 866–68 (6th Cir. 2017) (finding no custody during an interrogation that occurred in an exam room in a clinic where the defendant worked because she was familiar with the room in which it occurred, questioning was short and nonthreatening, and agents did not restrict her freedom to leave).

191 Sprosty v. Buchler, 79 F.3d 635 (7th Cir.), *cert. denied*, 519 U.S. 854 (1996).

192 *Id.* at 643.

193 United States v. Quinn, 815 F.2d 153, 154–56 (1st Cir. 1987).

place near his home, he was in his car viewable by the public, and was repeatedly told that he was not under arrest and was free to leave.[194] Thus, the number of officers present is only one of many factors to be considered when applying the totality-of-the-circumstances test for custody.

5. The Duration and Character of the Interrogation

Several factors concerning the circumstances under which an interrogation occurred can provide insights into whether someone was in custody for *Miranda* purposes during the encounter. The following subsections explore nine such characteristics that commonly occur. These nine situations are not, however, an exclusive list of the factors that might indicate custody or a lack thereof.

a. Focus of the Investigation

Miranda is generally understood to have abandoned the "focus of investigation" test of *Escobedo* to determine when an interrogated suspect is entitled to warnings. In *Beckwith v. United States*, the defendant had become the focus of a criminal tax investigation by the time he was interviewed by IRS agents at his home. The U.S. Supreme Court specifically held that even though a suspect is the focus of a criminal investigation, the suspect need not be given *Miranda* warnings if the suspect is not otherwise in custody or deprived of freedom of action in any significant way.[195]

The focus concept may still have some vitality, however, as one of the circumstances to be considered in determining the custody issue, but only if an officer's views or beliefs are somehow manifested to the person under interrogation and affect how a reasonable person in that position perceives his or her freedom to leave:

> An officer's knowledge or beliefs may bear upon the custody issue if they are conveyed, by word or deed, to the individual being questioned. . . .Those beliefs are relevant only to the extent they would affect how a reasonable person in the position of the individual being questioned would gauge the breadth of his or her "freedom of

---

[194] United States v. Wright, 777 F.3d 769, 777 (5th Cir. 2015).

[195] Beckwith v. United States, 425 U.S. 341 (1976).

action . . . ." Even a clear statement from an officer that the person under interrogation is a prime suspect is not, in itself, dispositive of the custody issue, for some suspects are free to come and go until the police decide to make an arrest. The weight and pertinence of any communications regarding the officer's degree of suspicion will depend upon the facts and circumstances of the particular case.[196]

b. Investigative *Terry* Stops and Traffic Stops

In *Berkemer v. McCarty*, the U.S. Supreme Court held that ordinary *Terry*-type investigative stops of people or vehicles are noncustodial for *Miranda* purposes because they are brief, take place in public, and typically involve only one or two officers.[197] Accordingly, they do not require *Miranda* warnings—even during traffic stops involving the investigation of driving under the influence, as was the case in *Berkemer* itself. *Pennsylvania v. Bruder* applied *Berkemer* to a case in which "a single police officer ask[ed] [a suspect] a modest number of questions and request[ed] him to perform a simple balancing test at a location visible to passing motorists."[198] The U.S. Supreme Court reaffirmed that *Miranda* warnings are not needed under such circumstances.

c. Time of Interrogation

The hour at which an interrogation takes place may also be an important factor in determining if someone is in custody for *Miranda* purposes. Questioning conducted during business hours is less likely to be considered custodial than is an interrogation conducted in the late evening or early morning.[199]

d. Duration of Interrogation

"Relay" interrogations that last for hours are likely to indicate that the suspect was in custody, especially if the suspect was denied food, water,

---

[196] Stansbury v. California, 511 U.S. 318, 325 (1994).

[197] Berkemer v. McCarty, 468 U.S. 420 (1984).

[198] *Id.*; Pennsylvania v. Bruder, 488 U.S. 9, 11 (1988).

[199] Orozco v. Texas, 394 U.S. 324, 325–26 (1969) (finding the suspect was in custody in his home because several officers interrogated him at 4:00 A.M.); United States v. Mittel-Carey, 493 F.3d 36, 39–40 (1st Cir. 2007) (finding custody at home when questioning occurred at 6:25 A.M.).

bathroom breaks, or rest during a so-called marathon questioning session. Such tactics, as discussed earlier, may also violate due process.[200]

e. Presence of Other Persons

Miranda expressly indicated a concern for *incommunicado* interrogations, those in which suspects are "cut off from the outside world."[201] Thus, interrogations of suspects conducted in the presence of family, friends, or neutral persons are more likely to be considered noncustodial than those in which access to others is permitted.[202] For example, the court in *United States v. Azua-Rinconda* found that the defendant had not been in custody for *Miranda* purposes even though officers had not informed him that he was free to leave, largely because the encounter took place mid-morning in the defendant's home and he was able to sit with his fiancée during questioning. [203]

Conversely, deliberately removing a suspect from the presence of family, friends, and other people indicates custody. *United States v. Griffin*, for instance, held that a suspect was in custody in his home when police sent his parents away and did not allow the suspect to leave the room in which he was being questioned unless they escorted him.[204]

f. Probation and Parole Interviews

People on probation or parole, although subject to numerous restrictive conditions governing various aspects of life, are not in custody for *Miranda* purposes simply because of their correctional status. Many such interviews, unlike custodial arrest situations, are often arranged by appointment at mutually convenient times and are conducted in familiar, nonintimidating surroundings. Such meetings do not become custodial for *Miranda* purposes because a probation or parole officer can compel attendance and demand truthful answers at the interview.[205] Nonetheless,

---

200 Davis v. North Carolina, 384 U.S. 737 (1966); Ashcraft v. Tennessee, 322 U.S. 143 (1944).

201 Miranda v. Arizona, 384 U.S. 436, 445 (1966).

202 *See, e.g.*, People v. Butterfield, 65 Cal. Rptr. 765 (Cal. App. 1968).

203 United States v. Azua-Rinconda, 914 F.3d 319, 326–27 (4th Cir. 2019).

204 United States v. Griffin, 922 F.2d 1343 (8th Cir. 1990).

205 Minnesota v. Murphy, 465 U.S. 420 (1984).

such interviews can become custodial if other indicia of arrest are present. For instance, the court in *United States v. Barnes* determined that a person on parole had been in custody during an interrogation because his meeting with three officers was unscheduled, was conducted under threat of parole revocation, and officers confronted him with adversarial evidence.[206]

g. Execution of Search Warrants

In the absence of other factors indicating custody such as physical restraint, a person who is detained "during the execution of a search warrant is normally not in custody for *Miranda* purposes."[207] But indicia of arrest can make such a situation custodial. For instance, a court ruled that the defendant in *United States v. Hashime* was in custody during the execution of a search warrant at his home for the following reasons:[208]

> Hashime had awoken at gunpoint to a harrowing scene: his house was occupied by a flood of armed officers who proceeded to evict him and his family and restrict their movements once let back inside. Throughout the interrogation, Hashime was isolated from his family members, with his mother's repeated requests to see him denied. It is little wonder that Hashime testified that, during the interrogation, "I didn't think I had any chance to leave. . . . I felt that I was . . . trapped and . . . had to stay where I was and do what I was told."[209]

In *United States v. Kim*, the court held the defendant was in custody when she was questioned during the search of a store given other indicia of arrest.[210] Not only did the police control over the store during the search create a police-dominated environment, but also the police treatment of the defendant would have led any reasonable person to feel as if he or she were under arrest.[211] For one thing, the defendant was locked in the store and, therefore, was not free to leave. Also, the defendant's husband and

---

206 United States v. Barnes, 713 F.3d 1200, 1204–06 (9th Cir. 2013).

207 United States v. Saadeh, 61 F.3d 510, 520 (7th Cir. 1995); *see also* Michigan v. Summers, 452 U.S. 692 (1981).

208 United States v. Hashime, 734 F.3d 278, 283–85 (4th Cir. 2013).

209 *Id.* at 284.

210 United States v. Kim, 292 F.3d 969 (9th Cir. 2002).

211 *Id.* at 977.

another relative tried to join her in the store, but police kept them apart, thereby physically isolating her "from two family members who could have provided both moral support and, given her limited English, a more complete understanding of the overall situation."[212]

h. The Language Used to Summon the Suspect

The language used by police to summon, a suspect can be an ambiguous factor. Language is generally relevant to custody determinations only to the extent that language communicates custody or coercion. For example, when police tell a suspect, "you're under arrest," or "stay here and don't move," such language unambiguously indicates that the suspect is in custody. But what if an officer were to say, "you should not leave" or "if you know what's good for you, you will stay and tell me everything I want to know"?[213] Because such statements may or may not indicate custody, wise law enforcement officers will give *Miranda* warnings to prevent the possible exclusion of statements secured after such language is used.

The language used to summon someone for questioning is particularly important in cases in which the person being questioned is an inmate in a jail or prison. For example, in *Arthur v. State*, the court found that a detainee at a correctional work release center was in custody for *Miranda* purposes when he had been summoned by his shift supervisor and questioned concerning a discrepancy in the inmate's reported work hours and the earnings he reported to correctional authorities.[214] However, when inmates are told that they do not need to speak with the officials seeking to question them, or that they are "free" to leave the interrogation and return to their normal routine within the correctional facility, courts usually find that any statements made during such questioning were noncustodial.[215]

---

212 *Id.*

213 Katherine M. Swift, *Drawing a Line Between* Terry *and* Miranda: *The Degree and Duration of Restraint*, 73 U. CHI. L. REV. 1075, 1093 (2006).

214 Arthur v. State, 575 So. 2d 1165, 1189 (Ala. Ct. Crim. App. 1990).

215 State v. Owen, 510 N.W.2d 503 (Neb. Ct. App. 1993).

i. The Extent to Which the Suspect Is Confronted with Evidence of Guilt

Confronting a suspect with evidence of guilt does not usually transform a noncustodial interrogation into a custodial one. Still, how such confrontations occur can nonetheless indicate police coercion which can, in turn, give rise to a finding that a suspect was in custody as illustrated by *United States v. Beraun-Panez.*[216] In that case, police separated the defendant from his co-worker in a remote rural location and then repeatedly accused him of lying, confronted him with false or misleading witness statements, and employed "good cop–bad cop" interrogation tactics. They also put the defendant in fear of deportation, consistently "insisting on the 'truth' until he told them what they sought," thereby establishing "a setting from which a reasonable person would believe that he or she was not free to leave."[217]

Conversely, when police do not confront a suspect with evidence of guilt, such a factor weighs against a finding of custody. In *United States v. Cazares*, for example, the court found the defendant was not in custody despite having been placed in a small interrogation room with several officers present.[218] The court reasoned that officers had told the defendant he was not under arrest, used neutral language when questioning him, and did not confront the defendant with evidence of guilt.

j. Whether the Suspect Initiated Contact with the Police

If a suspect summons the police, initiates an interview, or both, a court is likely to hold a subsequent interrogation noncustodial.[219] In *United States v. Jonas*, for instance, the defendant learned indirectly that an FBI agent wanted to contact him.[220] He called the agent, agreed to talk with the

---

216 United States v. Beraun-Panez, 812 F.2d 578 (9th Cir. 1987).

217 *Id.* at 580.

218 United States v. Cazares, 788 F.3d 956, 981 (9th Cir. 2015).

219 *See, e.g.*, Saleh v. Fleming, 512 F.3d 548, 551 (9th Cir. 2008) (finding no custody during an inmate's phone call with a police investigator because the defendant had initiated the call and was free to end it at any time simply by hanging up).

220 United States v. Jonas, 786 F.2d 1019 (11th Cir. 1986).

FBI, and appeared voluntarily at FBI offices. The interview was held to be noncustodial.

B. Interrogation

The *Miranda* requirements apply only if a person in custody is subjected to interrogation. In this context, **interrogation** is a broad term that encompasses more than express questioning. It includes any "words or actions on the part of [law enforcement] . . . that the[y] should know are reasonably likely to elicit an incriminating response from the suspect."[221] The Supreme Court has defined an *incriminating response* as "any response—whether inculpatory or exculpatory—that the prosecution may seek to introduce at trial."[222]

Reasonable people might differ as to whether particular conduct constitutes conduct that is likely to elicit an incriminating response. Consider the majority and dissenting opinions in the U.S. Supreme Court's decision in *Rhode Island v. Innis*.[223]

Innis involved a murder suspect who had been taken into custody by the police. After he was given *Miranda* warnings, he invoked his right to counsel. While transporting the defendant, the police asked him no direct questions. However, they did talk among themselves about how unfortunate it was that they did not find the murder weapon in the case because the crime scene was near a school for children with disabilities. One officer said to another, "[T]here's a lot of handicapped children running around in this area, and God forbid one of them might find a weapon with shells and they might hurt themselves." Another officer responded: "[I]t would be too bad if a little girl would pick up the gun, maybe kill herself."[224] At that point, the suspect interrupted the police officers' conversation and told them that he would show them where he had hidden the gun. The U.S. Supreme Court first clarified that *Miranda* is implicated even when police do not directly question suspects; certain

---

221 Rhode Island v. Innis, 446 U.S. 291, 301 (1980).

222 *Id.* at 302 n.5.

223 *Id.* at 291.

224 *Id.* 294–95.

"techniques of persuasion" in a custodial setting can amount to the equivalent of interrogation.[225]

> *Miranda* safeguards come into play whenever a person in custody is subjected to either express questioning or its functional equivalent. That is to say, the term "interrogation" under *Miranda* refers not only to express questioning, but also to any words or actions on the part of the police (other than those normally attendant to arrest and custody) that the police should know are reasonably likely to elicit an incriminating response from the suspect. The latter portion of this definition focuses primarily upon the perceptions of the suspect, rather than the intent of the police. This focus reflects the fact that the *Miranda* safeguards were designed to vest a suspect in custody with an added measure of protection against coercive police practices, without regard to objective proof of the underlying intent of the police.[226]

The Court, however, was sharply divided as to whether the officers' conversation in *Innis* was the functional equivalent of interrogation. A majority held it was not, reasoning that the conversation in question amounted to "nothing more than a dialogue between the two officers to which no response from the respondent was invited."[227]

> [I]t cannot be fairly concluded that the respondent was subjected to the "functional equivalent" of questioning. It cannot be said, in short, that [the officers] should have known that their conversation was reasonably likely to elicit an incriminating response from the respondent. There is nothing in the record to suggest that the officers were aware that the respondent was peculiarly susceptible to an appeal to his conscience concerning the safety of handicapped children. Nor is there anything in the record to suggest that the police knew that the respondent was unusually disoriented or upset at the time of his arrest . . . .
>
> Given the fact that the entire conversation appears to have consisted of no more than a few off-hand remarks, we cannot say that the officers should have known that it was reasonably likely that Innis would so respond. This is not a case where the police carried on a lengthy harangue

[225] *Id.* at 299.

[226] *Id.* at 300–01.

[227] *Id.* at 302.

> in the presence of the suspect. Nor does the record support the respondent's contention that, under the circumstances, the officers' comments were particularly "evocative."[228]

The defendant's incriminating statements in *Innis* as to where he had hidden the gun were therefore admissible.

The dissent in *Innis*, however, argued that the officers had engaged in the functional equivalent of interrogation:

> One can scarcely imagine a stronger appeal to the conscience of a suspect—any suspect—than the assertion that if the weapon is not found an innocent person will be hurt or killed. And not just any innocent person, but an innocent child—a little girl—a helpless, handicapped little girl on her way to school. The notion that such an appeal could not be expected to have any effect unless the suspect were known to have some special interest in handicapped children verges on the ludicrous. As a matter of fact, the appeal to a suspect to confess for the sake of others, to "display some evidence of decency and honor," is a classic interrogation technique.[229]

1. The "Functional Equivalent" of Interrogation

The following cases illustrate situations in which courts have found the actions of police to constitute the functional equivalent of interrogation: coached lineups, reverse lineups, and psychiatric examinations.

a. Coached Lineups

In *Innis*, the Supreme Court said that "the use of lineups in which a coached witness would pick the defendant as the perpetrator" would constitute the functional equivalent of interrogation.[230] The Court reasoned that the practice was "designed to establish that the defendant was, in fact, guilty as a predicate for further interrogation."[231]

---

[228] *Id.* at 302–03.

[229] *Id.* at 305 (Marshall, J., dissenting) (quoting FRED E. INBAU & JOHN E. REID, CRIMINAL INTERROGATION AND CONFESSIONS 60–62 (2d ed. 1967)).

[230] *Id.* at 299.

[231] *Id.*

b. Reverse Lineups

The *Innis* Court also said that the use of so-called reverse lineups was the functional equivalent of interrogation. A reverse lineup is a practice "in which a defendant would be identified by coached witnesses as the perpetrator of a fictitious crime, with the object of inducing him to confess to the actual crime of which he was suspected in order to escape the false prosecution."[232] A variation on reverse lineups was also held to be the functional equivalent of interrogation in *In re Durand*, a case in which the police showed the suspect police reports of other crimes to which they did not believe the suspect to be connected.[233] The court stated that the officers "should have known that showing the defendant the police reports was likely to elicit an incriminating response from the defendant."[234]

c. Psychiatric Examinations

In *Estelle v. Smith*, the U.S. Supreme Court held that psychiatric examinations constitute interrogations for *Miranda* purposes because the responses to the questions asked of the defendant during such an examination could be introduced at trial against the defendant.[235] *Miranda* warnings are even required before a psychiatric examination for in-custody defendants who raise a defense related to mental illness.[236] That being said, the typical limits on the use of unwarned statements apply. Thus, for example, although statements defendants make during psychiatric examinations that occur without *Miranda* warnings cannot be used in the prosecution's case-in-chief, they can be used for impeachment purposes or even to rebut psychiatric evidence introduced by the defense.[237]

---

232 *Id.*

233 *In re* Durand, 293 N.W.2d 383 (Neb. 1980).

234 *Id.* at 420.

235 Estelle v. Smith, 451 U.S. 454 (1981).

236 Rosen v. Superintendent Mahanoy SCI, 972 F.3d 245, 260 (3d Cir. 2020).

237 *See, e.g.*, United States v. Coonce, 932 F.3d 623, 636 (8th Cir. 2019); Penry v. Johnson, 215 F.3d 504, 509–11 (5th Cir. 2000), *rev'd on other grounds*, 532 U.S. 782 (2001); Hendricks v. Vasquez, 974 F.2d 1099, 1108 (9th Cir. 1992), *amended sub nom.* Hendricks v. Calderon, 70 F.3d 1032 (9th Cir. 1995).

By contrast, *Miranda* warnings are not required before psychiatric examinations that are designed to establish defendants' competency, rather than responsibility. For instance, in *Nguyen v. Garcia*, a federal appeals court held that *Miranda* warnings were not required before a psychiatric examination to determine a defendant's competency to stand trial because the results would be admissible only in the competency hearing, as opposed to allowing statements to be used by prosecution to establish guilt."[238] The court quoted from the U.S. Supreme Court's decision in *Medina v. California* when it said,

> In a competency hearing, the "emphasis is on [the defendant's] capacity to consult with counsel and to comprehend the proceedings, and . . . this is by no means the same test as those which determine criminal responsibility at the time of the crime."[239]

The court also noted that the purposes *Miranda* warnings serve are inapplicable to competency determinations:

> Not only are competency hearings entirely distinct in purpose from the guilt phase of trial, but competency hearings do not invoke the same concerns of self-incrimination—the right *Miranda* is designed to protect—that are relevant during the guilt and penalty phases of trial. The Fifth Amendment privilege against self-incrimination exists to prohibit the government from forcing the defendant to talk and then using the defendant's own statements to satisfy its burden of establishing guilt These concerns have no place at a competency hearing.[240]

The same logic applies to the psychiatric examination of juveniles to determine their competency to stand trial as adults.[241] Again, courts reason that such evaluations are designed to evaluate whether juveniles are fit to be transferred to adult court, rather than to incriminate the defendants.[242]

Finally, courts have similarly ruled that *Miranda* warnings are not required before psychiatric evaluations to determine defendants'

---

[238] Nguyen v. Garcia, 477 F.3d 716, 725–26 (9th Cir. 2007).

[239] *Id.* at 724 (quoting Medina v. California, 505 U.S. 437, 448 (1992)).

[240] *Id.* at 725 (citing Oregon v. Elstad, 470 U.S. 298, 304–05 (1985); Estelle v. Smith, 451 U.S. 454, 462 (1981)).

[241] *See* United States v. Juvenile Male, 554 F.3d 456 (4th Cir. 2009).

[242] *See, e.g.*, United States v. A.R., 38 F.3d 699, 703–04 (3d Cir. 1994).

competency to be sentenced.[243] Note, however, that if statements from such examinations are to be used as substantive evidence at a sentencing hearing, then *Miranda* warnings are likely necessary.[244]

2. Psychological Ploys Likely to Constitute "Functional" Interrogation

The *Innis* Court also mentioned the use of certain psychological ploys "such as to 'posi[t] the guilt of the subject,' to 'minimize the moral seriousness of the offense,' and 'to cast blame on the victim or on society'" as being "techniques of persuasion, no less than express questioning," that are the functional equivalent of interrogation in a custodial setting.[245] But determining which psychological ploys posit the guilt of the suspect and, therefore, are the functional equivalents of interrogation, and which ploys do not has proven to be a tricky venture.

These psychological ploys are considered to be the *functional equivalent of interrogation*: seeking a suspect's "cooperation," making pleas or directives to conscience, implying blame, confronting a suspect with evidence, and confronting a suspect with an accomplice.

a. Seeking a Suspect's "Cooperation"

Asking a suspect to cooperate in the investigation and implying that such cooperation would be beneficial to the suspect is the functional equivalent of interrogation because it is likely to elicit an incriminating response. This is especially true in cases in which police suggest that it is the "last chance" or "only chance" for a suspect to cooperate or to tell the suspect's side of the story.[246] For instance, telling a suspect that they must confess immediately or lose the opportunity to reduce their sentence by cooperating constitutes the functional equivalent of interrogation that triggers *Miranda*.[247] Similarly, lying about the penalties associated with the offense for which a suspect was arrested to incentivize that suspect's

---

243 Mahaffey v. Schomig, 294 F.3d 907, 919–20 (7th Cir. 2002).

244 Gardner v. Johnson, 247 F.3d 551, 557–58 (5th Cir. 2001).

245 Rhode Island v. Innis, 446 U.S. 291, 299 (1980).

246 *E.g.*, United States v. Padilla, 387 F.3d 1087 (9th Cir. 2004).

247 *See* United States v. Anderson, 929 F.2d 96, 100 (2d Cir. 1991).

cooperation also constitutes a psychological ploy that is the functional equivalent of interrogation.[248]

b. Making Pleas or Directives to the Conscience

Pleading with a suspect to "tell the truth" or "come clean" (or commanding the suspect to do so) is the functional equivalent of interrogation.[249] Accordingly, suspects are entitled to *Miranda* warnings before law enforcement officers make such appeals to suspects' consciences or religious beliefs.

c. Implying Blame

In *United States v. Rambo*, police began a discussion with the suspect by telling him "that much of the blame will fall on [his] shoulders."[250] The court ruled this was the very type of ploy that posits the guilt of the suspect that *Innis* specified would constitute the functional equivalent of interrogation.

d. Confronting Suspect with Evidence

Following *Innis*, most courts consider confronting a suspect with evidence of guilt to be the functional equivalent of interrogation. For example, in *Drury v. State*, an officer was investigating a burglary at a local convenience store in which magazines, cigarettes, liquor, and lottery tickets were stolen.[251] A tire iron that was used to pry open the door to the store was recovered from the inside of the store. A tip led the officer to call the defendant in for questioning. Once the suspect was in the stationhouse, and without having administered any *Miranda* warnings, the officer put the tire iron and a trash bag containing the stolen magazines on a table in front of the suspect and then told the suspect that the evidence would be tested for fingerprints.[252] In response, the suspect offered reasons why his fingerprint would be on both the tire iron and the magazines, making incriminating statements in the process. The court ruled that the

---

[248] United States v. Young, 964 F.3d 938, 943–44 (10th Cir. 2020).

[249] *See, e.g.*, United States v. Tyler, 164 F.3d 150 (3d Cir. 1998).

[250] United States v. Rambo, 365 F.3d 906, 909 (10th Cir. 2004).

[251] Drury v. State, 793 A.2d 567, 568–69 (Md.), *cert. denied*, 537 U.S. 942 (2002).

[252] *Id.* at 569.

officer had engaged in the functional equivalent of interrogation because the officer must have known that his conduct would be likely to elicit an incriminating response from the suspect.[253]

Courts treat the confronting witnesses with testimonial evidence, such as the statements of witnesses, in much the same way as they do physical evidence, like the tire iron and trash bag in *Drury*. For instance, in *Commonwealth v. DeJesus*, the Supreme Court of Pennsylvania held that an officer's having told the defendant that he had been implicated in shootings by two witnesses was the functional equivalent of interrogation.[254] The Hawaii Supreme Court reached the same conclusion in *State v. Uganiza*, a case in which police showed the defendant written statements of witnesses that implicated the defendant in the crime.[255]

It should be noted, however, that courts differentiate "confronting" a suspect with evidence against him or her from merely "informing" the person of such evidence. For example, in *State v. Bragg*, the Supreme Judicial Court of Maine ruled that an officer's statements to the defendant that her breath-test result was 0.13% blood alcohol content, and that the presumptive level of intoxication in Maine was 0.08%, were merely matter-of-fact communications about evidence that did not rise to level of "interrogation" for *Miranda* purposes.[256] Similarly, the court in *United States v. Benton*, determined that there was no psychological ploy to elicit an incriminating response when an officer "did nothing more than tell [the defendant] why he was being arrested."[257]

The line between "confronting" a suspect with evidence and merely "informing" the suspect about evidence is not always clear. For some courts, the distinction turns on whether law enforcement shared unsolicited information as opposed to responding to a question from the suspect. Consider *United States v. Thomas*, in which the defendant asked

---

253 *Id.* at 572.

254 Commonwealth v. DeJesus, 787 A.2d 394 (Pa. 2001), *abrogated on other grounds by* Commonwealth v. Cousar, 928 A.2d 1025 (Pa. 2007).

255 State v. Uganiza, 702 P.2d 1352 (Haw. 1985).

256 State v. Bragg, 48 A.3d 769 (Me. 2012).

257 United States v. Benton, 996 F.2d 642, 644 (3d Cir. 1993).

an agent a question about the evidence against her.[258] He responded to the question by explaining the evidence they had obtained which contradicted her alibi. She then made incriminating statements. She sought to have those statements suppressed, arguing that the agent knew his recitation of the evidence was likely to elicit an incriminating response and, therefore, was the functional equivalent of interrogation. A federal appeals court acknowledged that providing unsolicited information to suspects concerning the evidence against them may constitute interrogation, but differentiated that from responding to a request for such information.[259]

e. Confronting a Suspect with an Accomplice

Nelson v. Fulcomer held that "confronting a suspect with his alleged partner in crime and the fact that the partner has confessed is precisely the kind of psychological ploy that *Innis*'s definition of interrogation was designed to prohibit."[260] However, when suspects ask for the source of information against them and are then presented with the inculpatory statements of victims, witnesses, or accomplices, courts generally hold that such suspects were not subjected to interrogation or its functional equivalent.[261]

3. Psychological Ploys Unlikely to Constitute "Functional" Interrogation

The following psychological ploys are generally not the functional equivalent of interrogation: directly responding to questions, allowing a suspect to talk with friends or family, and placing suspects in the same location as other suspects.

a. Directly Responding to Questions

As previously mentioned, when suspects ask law enforcement questions about the reasons for their arrests or for information concerning the crimes for which they are being investigated, courts generally hold that

---

258 United States v. Thomas, 11 F.3d 1392 (7th Cir. 1993).

259 *Id.* at 1397.

260 Nelson v. Fulcomer, 911 F.2d 928 (3d Cir. 1990).

261 Roth v. State, 788 A.2d 101 (Del. 2001).

the responses to suspect-initiated questions are not the functional equivalent of interrogation for *Miranda* purposes. In *United States v. Taylor*, for example, police arrested the defendant on drug possession charges.[262] During the arrest, she asked the police, "Why is this happening to me?" An officer replied, "You can't be growing dope on your property like that."[263] In response, the woman made a series of incriminating statements. The court ruled that the officer's comment in response to her initial question was not a psychological ploy designed to get the defendant to make an incriminating statement, but rather was a direct response to her question.[264]

b. Allowing a Suspect to Talk with Friends or Family

Under the U.S. Supreme Court's decision in *Arizona v. Mauro*, law enforcement might hope that by allowing a suspect to talk with friends or family a suspect might then say something incriminating, but that hope—without more—is insufficient to constitute the functional equivalent of interrogation.[265] The defendant in *Mauro* was in custody on suspicion of murdering his son. He indicated that he did not wish to be questioned further without a lawyer present; police honored that request by ending their questioning of the suspect.[266] The defendant's wife, who was being questioned in another room, asked to speak to her husband. They were allowed to speak, but an officer was present in the room, and the conversation was tape-recorded with the couple's knowledge.[267]

The husband's defense at trial was that he had been insane at the time he killed his son. To show that he was not insane, the state played a recording of the conversation between the defendant and his wife. At trial, the defendant argued that allowing the spouses to meet together constituted a psychological ploy designed to elicit an incriminating response. Since he had already invoked his right to counsel, he therefore

---

262 United States v. Taylor, 985 F.2d 3 (1st Cir. 1993).

263 *Id.* at 6.

264 *Id.* at 8; *see also* United States v. Briggs, 273 F.3d 737 (7th Cir. 2001).

265 Arizona v. Mauro, 481 U.S. 520 (1987).

266 *Id.* at 522.

267 *Id.* at 522–23.

argued such a ploy rendered his statements inadmissible under *Miranda*. The trial court disagreed. Reasoning that the meeting "was not a ruse, nor a subterfuge by the police. They did not create this situation [i.e., allowing the meeting] as an indirect means of avoiding the dictates of *Miranda*."[268] The court noted that the police were worried about the safety of the couple, as well as whether they would "cook up a lie or swap statements with each other that shouldn't have been allowed, and whether some escape attempt might have been made, or whether there might have been an attempt to smuggle in a weapon. They had no idea what to expect along those lines."[269]

The defendant successfully appealed his conviction to the Arizona Supreme Court, but the U.S. Supreme Court reversed, thereby upholding the trial court's ruling that the actions of the police were not the functional equivalent of police interrogation:

> There is no evidence that the officers sent Mrs. Mauro in to see her husband for the purpose of eliciting incriminating statements. As the trial court found, the officers tried to discourage her from talking to her husband, but finally "yielded to her insistent demands . . . ." Nor was Detective Manson's presence improper. His testimony, that the trial court found credible, indicated a number of legitimate reasons—not related to securing incriminating statements—for having a police officer present . . . . Finally, the weakness of Mauro's claim that he was interrogated is underscored by examining the situation from his perspective . . . .
>
> The Arizona Supreme Court was correct to note that there was a "possibility" that Mauro would incriminate himself while talking to his wife. It also emphasized that the officers were aware of that possibility when they agreed to allow the Mauros to talk to each other. But the actions in this case were far less questionable than the "subtle compulsion" that we held not to be interrogation in *Innis* . . . . Officers do not interrogate a suspect simply by hoping that he will incriminate himself.[270]

---

[268] *Id.* at 524 (quoting the record from the trial court proceeding).

[269] *Id.* at 523–24.

[270] *Id.* at 528–29.

Whitehead v. Cowan illustrates how courts have applied *Mauro*.[271] That case involved a situation in which police left an arrested suspect alone with a female acquaintance. Outside police presence and, importantly, with no encouragement from the police, the acquaintance convinced the defendant to confess to her. Relying on *Mauro*, the court in *Whitehead* ruled that even if the police had hoped that the defendant might make incriminating statements to the woman, their mere "hope" that he might do so was not deemed to be a sufficient psychological ploy to render their actions the functional equivalent of interrogation.[272] Courts have even applied this logic to situations in which law enforcement, hoping for a confession, placed an accomplice in the same cell as the defendant.[273] Note, however, that although this does not constitute the functional equivalent of interrogation for *Miranda*/Fifth Amendment purposes, such actions could violate the Sixth Amendment as discussed in Chapter 10.

c. Placing Suspects in the Same Location with Other Suspects

As mentioned in the previous section, for *Miranda*/Fifth Amendment purposes, "simply placing two individuals or suspects in the same area does not focus the police attention on a suspect in such a way that the suspect necessarily would feel added pressure . . . to say something" and, therefore, is not considered to be the functional equivalent of interrogation.[274] In *United States v. Vasquez*, the defendants were convicted of conspiracy to smuggle cocaine, among other drug-related crimes.[275] While customs officials screened the defendants separately upon arrival of a flight from Venezuela to Puerto Rico, agents became suspicious of their behavior and response to routine questions such that they decided both men should undergo secondary screening.[276] When the

---

271 Whitehead v. Cowan, 263 F.3d 708 (7th Cir. 2001).

272 *Id.* at 718–19.

273 United States v. Alexander, 447 F.3d 1290, 1295–97 (10th Cir. 2006).

274 United States v. Vazquez, 857 F.2d 857, 862 (1st Cir. 1988); *see also Alexander*, 447 F.3d at 1295–97.

275 *Vazquez*, 857 F.2d at 858.

276 *Id.* at 858–59.

men were placed in the same room, one made incriminating statements and, subsequently, implicated a third person on their flight.

Applying *Mauro*, a federal appeals court upheld their convictions over defense arguments that placing the men together was a ploy constituting the functional equivalent of interrogation.[277] The court noted, however, that the facts of the case presented a close call:

> In this case, at least some of the officials knew that Vazquez and Pizarro were providing inconsistent stories about their relationship. Thus, it could be argued that the customs agents should have known that the conflicting stories would make Vazquez feel unusually pressured when confronting Pizarro to say something that would persuade the authorities that he did not know Pizarro. In addition, unlike in *Mauro*, the authorities here could be reasonably sure of the nature of the comments likely to be made by the suspect and his possible associate—comments concerning their relationship that would be directly relevant to Vazquez's guilt or innocence. In *Mauro*, where the two individuals were husband and wife and there was no previous conflict in their statements to police officers, it arguably was less likely that any conversation would be directly relevant to the suspect's guilt or innocence, and thus "incriminating." In *Mauro*, the couple would be just as likely to discuss personal matters.
>
> These differences put this case much closer to the *Miranda* line than was *Mauro*. Nevertheless, we conclude that bringing together—*in an otherwise non-coercive setting*—two suspects who have given authorities conflicting stories is not sufficiently likely to elicit an incriminating response to meet the legal standard of "interrogation." In this case, the record shows a sudden, spontaneous exchange between Vazquez and Pizarro as soon as Vazquez was brought into the supervisor's office. There is no suggestion that the customs agents thrust Vazquez in front of Pizarro in an effort to "elicit" a comment from either of them. Nor is there evidence of any other tactic designed to encourage Vazquez or Pizarro to erupt upon meeting. This room was neither packed full of hostile officers glaring at Vazquez nor was there evidence that the officers had primed Vazquez for the meeting by expressly suggesting that he confront Pizarro head-on.[278]

---

[277] *Id.* at 863.

[278] *Id.* (italics in original).

Thus, if two suspects find themselves being detained in the same location that does not involve any elements of coercion, and they make incriminating statements that are overheard by police, police may benefit from what they overhear because *Innis*'s functional equivalent of interrogation test is not satisfied merely by placing two suspects together in the same location.

d. "Invitations" to Talk

Courts are divided on whether invitations to discuss a case constitute the functional equivalent of interrogation. *United States v. Rambo* held that a police officer's repeatedly saying, "If you want to talk to me about this stuff, that's fine" was the functional equivalent of interrogation.[279] But as previously mentioned, that case also involved the officer then confronting the suspect with evidence of guilt. But comparison, *Commonwealth v. D'Entremont* ruled that a police officer's having told a suspect in custody that she would be willing to speak with him about the case was not the functional equivalent of interrogation.[280] The court reasoned that even though the officer's invitation "struck a responsive chord," it merely constituted "an expression of her availability if [the defendant] wanted to talk."[281]

4. Statements That Are Beyond the Reach of *Miranda*

Although the definition of interrogation is broad, many situations fall outside the definition or fall within well-recognized exceptions to rules regarding interrogation and its functional equivalent.

a. Volunteered Statements

The most obvious situation not constituting interrogation is a volunteered statement—a statement made of a person's own volition and not in response to questioning by a law enforcement officer. Volunteered statements sometimes occur when a person—either intentionally or unintentionally—makes an incriminating statement in the presence of a

---

[279] United States v. Rambo, 365 F.3d 906, 909–10 (10th Cir. 2004).

[280] Commonwealth v. D'Entremont, 632 N.E.2d 1239 (Mass. App. Ct. 1994).

[281] *Id.* at 1242–43.

law enforcement officer. *United States v. Wright* found no interrogation when the defendant, standing in the doorway to his bedroom while it was being legally searched and without any provocation by police, admitted that he had purchased a rifle.[282]

Volunteered statements occur more frequently, however, when a person is in custody. For example, during a homicide arrest in *People v. Jenkins*, the arresting officer told the suspect that he was being arrested for killing a woman.[283] Unprompted, the suspect responded, "The bitch needed killing." The statement was held to be admissible as a volunteered, spontaneously made statement.

Volunteered statements can even obviate the need for *Miranda* warnings under circumstances in which they are normally required. For example, despite the fact that *Miranda* warnings are generally required before a defendant undergoes any court-ordered psychiatric examinations, the court in *Beaty v. Stewart* held they were not required because the defendant spontaneously volunteered incriminating statements to a psychiatrist[284] The psychiatrist testified that he was not questioning the defendant at the time the defendant spontaneously confessed; indeed, their session had ended and the two were just casually chatting when the defendant made statements that "came 'more or less out of the blue'" in a manner that the psychiatrist found "somewhat shocking."[285]

Law enforcement officers need not interrupt a volunteered statement to warn a suspect of *Miranda* rights. The *Miranda* opinion specifically said that "[t]here is no requirement that police stop a person who enters a police station and states that he wishes to confess to a crime, or a person who calls the police to offer a confession or any other statement he desires to make."[286]

---

[282] United States v. Wright, 991 F.2d 1180 (4th Cir. 1993).

[283] People v. Jenkins, 268 N.E.2d 198, 199 (Ill. App. Ct. 1971).

[284] Beaty v. Stewart, 303 F.3d 975, 991 (9th Cir. 2002).

[285] *Id.*

[286] Miranda v. Arizona, 384 U.S. 436, 478 (1966).

b. Clarifying Questions

Because many volunteered statements are ambiguous, an officer may try to clarify what is being said. A voluntary statement will not be judged to have evolved into an interrogation "simply because an officer, in the course of [the suspect's] narration, asks [him] to explain or clarify something he has already said voluntarily."[287] Thus, a statement will continue to be viewed as one that was purely volunteered even if the police asked some clarifying questions. But to qualify as truly clarifying questions, the questions cannot be directed toward expanding on the person's original statement in an attempt to enhance the suspect's guilt. Rather, the question must merely be aimed at clearing up or explaining the statement. For example, in *People v. Savage*, a man walked into a police station and made what is known as a "threshold confession" when he said: "I done it; I done it; arrest me; arrest me."[288] An officer asked him what he had done, and he responded that he had killed his wife. Then the officer asked him how, and he replied, "With an axe, that's all I had." The court held that the officer merely asked clarifying questions that did not constitute interrogation; therefore, no *Miranda* warnings were required.

c. Routine Booking Questions

As part of routine booking procedures, police gather and record various identifying information about the suspect. These data normally include the suspect's name, address, age, weight, and physical description. Collectively, this is referred to as "routine booking information." Although seemingly innocuous, routine booking information can constitute incriminating evidence in some cases. For example, if a teenager is arrested for public intoxication, she will make an incriminating statement if she answers the question "How old are you?"[289]

---

[287] State v. Porter, 281 S.E.2d 377, 385 (N.C. 1981).

[288] People v. Savage, 242 N.E.2d 446, 447 (Ill. App. Ct. 1968).

[289] *See, e.g.*, United States v. Scott, 270 F.3d 30, 43 n.8 (1st Cir. 2001) (ruling that questions regarding the defendant's age and residence while the officer was holding the defendant's fake identification card were not within routine booking exception, but rather were designed to illicit incriminating responses).

In *Pennsylvania v. Muniz*, a police officer noticed that the defendant-driver had stopped his vehicle on the side of the road.[290] When the officer asked him if he needed help, the officer noticed the scent of alcohol on Muniz's breath. After the officer told him to remain parked until his condition improved, Muniz sped off when the officer got back to his patrol car. The officer then pulled Muniz over and asked him to complete three field sobriety tests, all of which Muniz failed. Muniz was then arrested and taken to a police station.[291]

At the station, Muniz was told he would be videotaped during the booking procedures, but he was not Mirandized. During booking, the officer asked Muniz for his name, address, weight, eye color, date of birth, and age. The officer also asked, "[D]o you know what the date was of your sixth birthday?"[292] Muniz replied that he did not know. Over the defense counsel's objections, the video and audio portions of the booking proceedings were entered into evidence at Muniz's trial for driving under the influence and Muniz was convicted. He appealed on the grounds that the evidence should have been excluded because the tests were incriminating and completed prior to Muniz having been given *Miranda* warnings.

The U.S. Supreme Court had previously decided that asking a suspect to participate in field sobriety tests or to take a blood-alcohol test was "not an interrogation within the meaning of *Miranda*."[293] The *Muniz* Court held that routine booking questions regarding the suspect's name, address, eye color, weight, date of birth, and age are not interrogation, and therefore fall outside *Miranda*, because the questions were not intended to elicit information for investigatory purposes, but rather are gathered for recordkeeping purposes.[294] Moreover, because evidence of slurred speech in response to such questions is not testimonial, it is also admissible even if *Miranda* warnings were not given.[295] A plurality of the *Muniz* Court,

---

290 Pennsylvania v. Muniz, 496 U.S. 582 (1990).

291 *Id.* at 585.

292 *Id.* at 586.

293 South Dakota v. Neville, 459 U.S. 553, 565 n.15 (1983).

294 *Muniz*, 496 U.S. at 591.

295 *Id.* at 590–92.

however, decided that the "sixth birthday" question constituted interrogation for *Miranda* purposes because it was designed to elicit an incriminating response.[296]

The routine questioning exception to *Miranda* does not apply when a police officer has reason to believe that a suspect's answer to a routine question may be self-incriminating. For instance, although asking a person his or her place of birth does not usually constitute interrogation, the same question assumes a completely different character when an Immigration and Customs Enforcement (ICE) agent asks it of a person suspected of being in the United States illegally. Thus, some courts have held that such a question constitutes interrogation for *Miranda* purposes.[297] Similarly, asking arrestees about their gang affiliations during booking, even if routine, constitutes interrogation in jurisdictions in which there are "comprehensive scheme[s] of penal statutes" targeting gang-related crimes.[298]

d. Spontaneous Questions

When law enforcement officers ask questions spontaneously—especially in response to some emergency, the questions might not be interrogation. In *People v. Morse*, correctional officers were called to a cell where they found a prisoner near death from strangling.[299] While tending to the injured inmate, they asked another prisoner about the incident and received incriminating replies. The court upheld the admissibility of those statements even though the inmate had not received *Miranda* warnings because the questions were asked spontaneously in the context of an emergency:

> In the case before us, the conversational episode took place in a time period of perhaps a few seconds and in a setting devoid of "inquisitorial techniques." Murkerson, although a uniformed deputy sheriff, was in

---

[296] *Id.* at 593–94.

[297] *See, e.g.*, United States v. Pacheco-Lopez, 531 F.3d 420, 424 (6th Cir. 2008); United States v. Henley, 984 F.2d 1040, 1042 (9th Cir. 1993); United States v. Parra, 2 F.3d 1058, 1068 (10th Cir. 1993); United States v. Gonzalez-Sandoval, 894 F.2d 1043 (9th Cir. 1990).

[298] *See* United States v. Williams, 842 F.3d 1143, 1147 (9th Cir. 2016).

[299] People v. Morse, 76 Cal. Rptr. 391, 452 P.2d 607 (Cal. 1969).

> fact a jailer whose duties at the time were custodial, not investigative. . . . The general atmosphere of the setting discloses a preoccupation on the officers' part with reviving the victim rather than with interrogating a suspect. Murkerson and his companion were kneeling by [the victim's] body outside defendant's locked cell; defendant was not in face-to-face conversation with them but lying on his bunk. The questions were put to him by Murkerson while the latter was desperately attempting to resuscitate the victim and were couched in a context of stupefied wonderment, not of incisive inquiry. The answers were offered immediately—one gets the impression almost laconically—without any pressure from the questioner. We cannot detect in such an exchange any of the marks of an accusatory process. We are satisfied that no process of interrogation had been undertaken.[300]

It should be noted that rulings upholding spontaneous questioning by law enforcement personnel are quite rare. Only a handful of cases have followed the lead of the court in *Morse* since it was decided in 1969. One involved police asking, "[i]s she dead?" when they came across a car parked on the side of a road and found an eighteen-year-old boy with blood on his hands lying on top of a girl's unclothed body.[301] The boy's response of, "[y]es, I guess so," was deemed admissible even though the police did not give him *Miranda* warnings before asking their spontaneous question.[302]

e. Questions Related to Public Safety

The more common type of spontaneous questions asked under exigent circumstances are those that concern public safety. In *New York v. Quarles*, a woman approach two police officers and told them she had just been raped and that her assailant had entered a nearby supermarket carrying a gun.[303] One of the officers entered the store and spotted the defendant, who matched the description given by the woman. The officer pursued the suspect with his drawn gun and ordered the suspect to stop and put his hands over his head. The officer then frisked him and

---

300 *Id.* at 397–98.

301 People v. Quicke, 455 P.2d 787, 790 (Cal. 1969).

302 *Id.* at 793.

303 New York v. Quarles, 467 U.S. 649 (1984).

discovered that he was wearing an empty shoulder holster. After handcuffing the defendant, the officer asked him where the gun was. He nodded toward some empty cartons and responded, "The gun is over there."[304] Although the defendant was in police custody when he made his statements, and the facts fell within the coverage of *Miranda*, the U.S. Supreme Court held that there was a public safety exception to the *Miranda* warning requirement:

> The police in this case, in the very act of apprehending a suspect, were confronted with the immediate necessity of ascertaining the whereabouts of a gun which they had every reason to believe the suspect had just removed from his empty holster and discarded in the supermarket. So long as the gun was concealed somewhere in the supermarket, with its actual whereabouts unknown, it obviously posed more than one danger to the public safety: An accomplice might make use of it or a customer or employee might later come upon it.

The Court concluded that the need for answers to questions in situations posing a threat to public safety outweighed the need to protect the Fifth Amendment's privilege against self-incrimination. Furthermore, the Court held that the availability of the public safety exception does not depend on the motivation of the individual officers involved. The Court recognized that in a spontaneous, emergency like the one in *Quarles*, most police officers act out of different, instinctive motives: a concern for their own safety and that of others, and, perhaps, the desire to obtain incriminating evidence from the suspect. A rigid adherence to the *Miranda* rules is not required when police officers ask questions reasonably prompted by a concern for public safety. Finally, the Court acknowledged that the public safety exception lessens the clarity of the *Miranda* rule, but expressed confidence that the police would instinctively respond appropriately in situations threatening public safety.

Courts construe the public safety exception narrowly, applying it only where there is "an objectively reasonable need to protect the police or the public from any immediate danger associated with [a] weapon."[305] Thus,

---

304 *Id.* at 652.

305 United States v. Mobley, 40 F.3d 688, 693 (4th Cir. 1994).

beyond admitting statements in response to unwarned questions concerning unsecured firearms,[306] courts have also upheld questions about bombs, knives, needles, or other items that could injure an officer while conducting a pat-down can qualify under the public safety exception to *Miranda*.[307] But when the immediate danger has passed, courts disfavor the use of the public safety exception. For example, if a suspect is handcuffed and there are no others present who could use a weapon, questions about the possession or location of such weapons need to be asked after *Miranda* warnings are given.[308]

f. Not Acting at Law Enforcement's Behest

As a rule, the *Miranda* warning requirements apply only to custodial interrogations conducted by state actors—governmental officials who act on behalf of the state. Certainly, law enforcement officers are state actors, but so are those people who act under their direction. So long as a private citizen is not acting in concert with law enforcement officials, incriminating statements made by a person in response to custodial interrogation by a private citizen are admissible in court despite a lack of prior warnings.[309] Thus, for instance, *Miranda* warnings are not required when medical personnel question people about the cause of certain conditions even though responses might incriminate the patient.[310] —

In *United States v. Kimbrough*, a court determined that *Miranda* warnings were not required when a mother questioned her son about drugs that police found in the family basement.[311] Normally, questioning by a parent does not involve state action and, therefore, does not implicate the Fifth Amendment. That holds true even if the parent is a law enforcement

---

[306] *See also* United States v. Basher, 629 F.3d 1161 (9th Cir. 2011).

[307] *See, e.g.*, United States v. Simpkins, 978 F.3d 1, 10–11 (1st Cir. 2020); United States v. Hodge, 714 F.3d 380, 387 (6th Cir. 2013); United States v. Webster, 162 F.3d 308, 332 (5th Cir. 1998).

[308] *See, e.g.*, United States v. Jackson, 544 F.3d 351, 360 n.9 (1st Cir. 2008); United States v. Lim, 897 F.3d 673, 690–91 (5th Cir. 2018); *Mobley*, 40 F.3d at 693.

[309] *See* United States v. Romero, 897 F.2d 47 (2d Cir. 1990).

[310] United States v. Borchardt, 809 F.2d 1115, 1118–19 (5th Cir. 1987).

[311] United States v. Kimbrough, 477 F.3d 144, 151 (4th Cir. 2007).

agent, presuming that the parent is not involved in the investigation.[312] But if law enforcement officials enlist a parent to act on their behalf, questioning by such a parent likely constitutes state action triggering *Miranda*. By contrast, if police do not enlist a parent's help, but instead become the beneficiaries of the parent's independent actions, then such actions do not implicate *Miranda*. The court in *Kimbrough* determined the latter best described the situation in the case, but it was a close call:

> We cannot say that the officers should have known that showing Ms. Kimbrough the drugs in her house would coerce an incriminating response from her son. Indeed, there is no evidence in the record that the officers had any reason to believe that Ms. Kimbrough would confront [her son] at all. There is simply no evidence in the record that they knew or suspected that Ms. Kimbrough would ask officers to bring her son to the basement and then bombard him with questions. Although perhaps a fortuitous consequence from the officers' perspective, it was no more so than the situation in *Innis*, and the actions of the officers here were arguably less calculated. The officers' mere awareness of the possibility that showing Ms. Kimbrough the drugs might prompt her to speak to [her son], and, if so, that [he] might incriminate himself, does not constitute interrogation.[313] —

g. Interrogation by Undercover Agents

For Fifth Amendment purposes, conversations between suspects and undercover agents do not implicate *Miranda* because suspects cannot reasonably claim police compulsion from those they assume are not police agents. *Illinois v. Perkins* was a case in which police placed an undercover agent in a jail cell with a defendant who was incarcerated on charges unrelated to the murder that the agent was investigating.[314] When the undercover agent asked the defendant whether he had ever killed anyone, the defendant made statements implicating himself in the murder.[315] Because *Miranda*'s premise is that the danger of coercion results from the

---

312 Cook v. Warden, 677 F.3d 1133, 1140 (11th Cir. 2012).

313 *Kimbrough*, 477 F.3d at 151 (citing Rhode Island v. Innis, 446 U.S. 291, 302 (1980)).

314 Illinois v. Perkins, 496 U.S. 292 (1990).

315 *Id.* at 295.

interaction of custody and official interrogation, the *Perkins* Court rejected the argument that *Miranda* warnings were required whenever a suspect is technically in custody and converses with someone who happens to be a government agent. The Court reasoned that *Miranda* forbids coercion, not mere strategic deception by taking advantage of suspects' misplaced trust in those they believe to be fellow prisoners.[316]

> *Miranda* was not meant to protect suspects from boasting about their criminal activities in front of persons whom they believe to be their cellmates. This case is illustrative. Respondent had no reason to feel that undercover agent Parisi had any legal authority to force him to answer questions or that Parisi could affect respondent's future treatment. Respondent viewed the cellmate-agent as an equal and showed no hint of being intimidated by the atmosphere of the jail. In recounting the details of the Stephenson murder, respondent was motivated solely by the desire to impress his fellow inmates. He spoke at his own peril.[317]

C. Assertion of *Miranda* Rights Must Be Clear and Unambiguous

Unlike due process rights, which apply all the time, the rights guaranteed under the Self-Incrimination Clause of the Fifth Amendment must be invoked. Once in custody, suspects may invoke *Miranda* rights at any time prior to or during an interrogation, so long as they do so clearly and unambiguously so that a reasonable police officer under the circumstances would understand the suspect's intentions.[318]

1. No Particular Words Are Necessary

No particular words are required to invoke the Fifth Amendment right to remain silent. A suspect, therefore, does not need to use formal language like "I invoke my right to remain silent." Colloquialisms such as "I don't want to talk to you" would be sufficient. For example, in *Tice v. Johnson*, the court found that a suspect's statement that he "decided not to say any

---

[316] *Id.* at 296–97.

[317] *Id.* at 298.

[318] Davis v. United States, 512 U.S. 452 (1994).

more" was sufficient to invoke his Fifth Amendment rights.[319] And *United States v. Abdallah* held that *Miranda* was violated after questioning continued after the defendant said he "wasn't going to say anything at all."[320]

2. Ambiguous Words

If a statement by a suspect is ambiguous or equivocal, most courts hold that the police have no duty to clarify the suspect's intent; they may proceed with the interrogation, although a few courts require police to clarify the defendant's wishes with respect to the request for counsel.[321] *Davis v. United States*, the leading U.S. Supreme Court precedent on this point, involved a suspect who said, "[m]aybe I should talk to a lawyer."[322] The Court held that statement was too ambiguous to qualify as a clear assertion of the right to counsel.

The following statements have also been held to be too ambiguous to qualify as an unequivocal assertion of the right to counsel:

- "So if I requested a lawyer, there would be one that would come right now?"[323]
- "Do you think I need a lawyer?"[324]
- "I think I should talk to a lawyer, what do you think?"[325]
- "I can have a lawyer present through all this, right?"[326]
- "It would be nice to have an attorney."[327]
- "I really should have a lawyer, huh?"[328]

---

[319] Tice v. Johnson, 647 F.3d 87, 97 (4th Cir. 2011).

[320] United States v. Abdallah, 911 F.3d 201, 214–15 (4th Cir. 2018).

[321] *See, e.g.*, United States v. Fouche, 833 F.2d 1284 (9th Cir. 1987), *cert denied*, 486 U.S. 1017 (1988).

[322] *Davis*, 512 U.S. at 455.

[323] United States v. Bezanson-Perkins, 390 F.3d 34, 36, 40 (1st Cir. 2004).

[324] Diaz v. Senkowski, 76 F.3d 61, 63 (2d Cir. 1996).

[325] United States v. Delaney, 443 F. App'x 122, 130 (6th Cir. 2011).

[326] United States v. Younger, 398 F.3d 1179, 1187–88 (9th Cir. 2005).

[327] Ledbetter v. Edwards, 35 F.3d 1062, 1070 (6th Cir. 1994).

[328] United States v. Mays, 683 F. App'x 427, 433 (6th Cir. 2017).

- "How can I do to get an attorney here because I don't have enough to afford one."[329]

Courts have split on the phrase, "I think I need a lawyer." Some hold this phrase is too ambiguous to invoke *Miranda* rights,[330] while others conclude the opposite.[331] Conversely, "[c]an you call my attorney" was determined to be a clear invocation of *Miranda* rights.[332]

Courts also require clear and unambiguous assertions of the right to remain silent. Thus, a suspect's statements that "I just don't think that I should say anything"; "I need somebody that I can talk to"; and "I am not sure if I should be talking to you"[333] were held to be too ambiguous to constitute valid invocations of *Miranda* rights.

3. No Creation of Ambiguity Where None Exists

Even though they are under no obligation to do so, police may attempt to clarify whether the suspect actually wants an attorney whenever a suspect makes an ambiguous or equivocal statement. However, if a suspect clearly and unambiguously invokes *Miranda* rights, courts will not allow an accused's responses to further interrogation to be used to cast retrospective doubt on the clarity of the initial request itself. In *Smith v. Illinois*, the U.S. Supreme Court said, "No authority, and no logic, permits the interrogator to proceed . . . on his own terms and as if the defendant had requested nothing, in the hope that the defendant might be induced to say something casting retrospective doubt on his initial statement that he wished to speak through an attorney or not at all."[334]

---

329 Subdiaz-Osorio v. Humphreys, 947 F.3d 434, 444 (7th Cir. 2020).

330 Burket v. Angelone, 208 F.3d 172, 197–98 (4th Cir. 2000).

331 Wood v. Ercole, 644 F.3d 83, 92 (2d Cir. 2011).

332 United States v. Hunter, 708 F.3d 938, 948 (7th Cir. 2013).

333 United States v. Plugh, 648 F.3d 118, 128 (2d Cir. 2011); Burket v. Angelone, 208 F.3d 172, 199 (4th Cir. 2000).

334 Smith v. Illinois, 469 U.S. 91, 99 (1984) (per curiam).

4. A Suspect's Behavior Must Be Consistent with Assertion of Rights

If a suspect clearly and unambiguously invokes *Miranda* rights but then acts in a manner inconsistent with the assertion of the rights, courts almost always hold that the suspect's assertion of *Miranda* rights was equivocal and, therefore, invalid. For example, in *United States v. Drapeau*, the suspect clearly stated that he "did not want to talk to agents" after he was advised of his *Miranda* rights.[335] Yet, he then made an unprompted offer to cooperate with the police, rendering his assertion of the right to remain silent ambiguous. Under such circumstances, the court held that the police could continue the interrogation without violating *Miranda*.

D. Silence Insufficient to Invoke Rights *Prior to* Custodial Interrogation

In a fractured, plurality opinion, the U.S. Supreme Court held in *Salinas v. Texas* that one must not merely be silent to invoke one's Fifth Amendment privilege against self-incrimination, at least in the context of *precustodial* police interrogation.[336] In other words, to invoke the right to remain silent in this context, one must ironically not be silent; rather, one must speak to communicate the intention of subsequently standing mute.

The Court summarized the facts of *Salinas* as follows:

> [T]wo brothers were shot and killed in their Houston home. There were no witnesses to the murders, but a neighbor who heard gunshots saw someone run out of the house and speed away in a dark-colored car. Police recovered six shotgun shell casings at the scene. The investigation led police to [Salinas], who had been a guest at a party the victims hosted the night before they were killed. Police visited [Salinas] at his home, where they saw a dark blue car in the driveway. He agreed to hand over his shotgun for ballistics testing and to accompany police to the station for questioning.

---

[335] United States v. Drapeau, 414 F.3d 869, 874 (8th Cir. 2005).

[336] Salinas v. Texas, 570 U.S. 178 (2013).

> [Salinas's] interview with the police lasted approximately one hour. All agree that the interview was noncustodial, and the parties litigated this case on the assumption that he was not read *Miranda* warnings. For most of the interview, petitioner answered the officer's questions. But when asked whether his shotgun "would match the shells recovered at the scene of the murder," [Salinas] declined to answer. Instead, [he] "looked down at the floor, shuffled his feet, bit his bottom lip, clenched his hands in his lap, and began to tighten up." After a few moments of silence, the officer asked additional questions, which petitioner answered.[337]

Salinas was subsequently charged with murder. He did not testify at his trial. But prosecutors argued that his silence in response to the officer's question concerning the shell casings suggested that he was guilty. Salinas was convicted and appealed. He argued that the prosecution's introduction of his silence violated this Fifth Amendment privilege against self-incrimination. The U.S. Supreme Court rejected this argument. The plurality opinion reasoned that Salinas' Fifth Amendment claim to protect his precustodial silence failed because Salinas did not *assert* his right to remain silent; rather, he *was* silent.

> [Salinas's] Fifth Amendment claim fails because he did not expressly invoke the privilege against self-incrimination in response to the officer's question. It has long been settled that the privilege "generally is not self-executing" and that a witness who desires its protection "must claim it." Although "no ritualistic formula is necessary in order to invoke the privilege," a witness does not do so by simply standing mute.

The four dissenting justices criticized the logic of the majority opinion for "undermining the basic protection that the Fifth Amendment provides" since, prior to the *Salinas* decision, the privilege against self-incrimination usually operated "to allow a citizen to remain silent when asked a question requiring an incriminatory answer."[338]

> To permit a prosecutor to comment on a defendant's constitutionally protected silence would put that defendant in an impossible predicament.

---

[337] *Id.* at 181–82.

[338] Kastigar v. United States, 406 U.S. 441, 461 (1972).

> He must either answer the question or remain silent. If he answers the question, he may well reveal, for example, prejudicial facts, disreputable associates, or suspicious circumstances—even if he is innocent. . . . If he remains silent, the prosecutor may well use that silence to suggest a consciousness of guilt. And if the defendant then takes the witness stand in order to explain either his speech or his silence, the prosecution may introduce, say for impeachment purposes, a prior conviction that the law would otherwise make inadmissible. Thus, where the Fifth Amendment is at issue, to allow comment on silence directly or indirectly can compel an individual to act as "a witness against himself"—very much what the Fifth Amendment forbids. . . . And that is similarly so whether the questioned individual, as part of his decision to remain silent, invokes the Fifth Amendment explicitly or implicitly, through words, through deeds, or through reference to surrounding circumstances.[339]

Time will tell if *Salina*'s "use it or lose it" approach to the privilege against self-incrimination proves workable. Several states, including Florida[340] and Pennsylvania,[341] have rejected its logic, holding that their state constitutions provide more protections than the plurality's pronouncement in *Salinas* says the Fifth Amendment provides.

In light of *Salinas*, it appears that the safest course of action for noncustodial suspects subject to policing questioning who do not wish their silence to be used against them—and who do not wish to waive their Fifth Amendment rights—should state, "I wish to remain silent" or similar words to that effect. It is also important to keep in mind that *Salinas* involved silence in the face of questioning that occurred before any arrest and before *Miranda* warnings were given. Warnings were, therefore, unnecessary because Salinas was not subject to custodial interrogation at the time.

---

339 *Salinas*, 570 U.S. at 195 (Breyer, J., dissenting) (internal citations omitted).

340 State v. Horwitz, 191 So. 3d 429, 441 (Fla. 2016).

341 Commonwealth v. Molina, 104 A.3d 430, 500 (2014).

Chapter 7:

Giving *Miranda* Warnings

As previously explained, law enforcement officers must provide *Miranda* warnings to all suspects before conducting custodial interrogations, regardless of whether the offense is a major felony or a minor misdemeanor. Law enforcement officers may not assume that suspects know their rights just because suspects have prior experience with the criminal justice system. Nor may police assume that a suspect has the financial means to be able to afford an attorney, and therefore think that they need not advise the suspect of the right to appointed counsel for a suspect who cannot afford an attorney. In fact, most courts require full *Miranda* warnings to be provided to all suspects regardless of how knowledgeable the suspects may be about their rights—even to suspects who are police officers or practicing attorneys.[342] *Miranda* does not apply, though, to any civil proceedings such as customs procedures, civil commitments, extradition proceedings, and license revocation proceedings.

A. Sufficiency of the Language Used in *Miranda* Warnings

Assuming that *Miranda* warnings are required because a person is being interrogated while in custody, the *Miranda* decision suggested language that law enforcement officers could use to satisfy the mandates of that decision.[343] But the Court made clear that the warnings need not be given in the exact form used in the *Miranda* decision itself, so long as the

---

342 *See, e.g.*, United States v. Street, 472 F.3d 1298 (11th Cir. 2006); United States v. Farinacci-Garcia, 551 F. Supp. 465 (D.P.R. 1982).

343 Miranda v. Arizona, 384 U.S. 436, 467–79 (1966).

procedures are "at least as effective [as *Miranda* warnings] in apprising accused persons of their [rights] and in assuring a continuous opportunity to exercise [them]."[344]

In *California v. Prysock*, the Court made it clear that no "talismanic incantation" of *Miranda* warnings is required; rather, all that is necessary is that the words used reasonably convey to a suspect his or her *Miranda* rights.[345] In *Florida v. Powell*, for example, the Court upheld the following warning:

> You have the right to remain silent. If you give up the right to remain silent, anything you say can be used against you in court. You have the right to talk to a lawyer before answering any of our questions. If you cannot afford to hire a lawyer, one will be appointed for you without cost and before any questioning. You have the right to use any of these rights at any time you want during this interview.[346]

The defendant in *Powell* challenged the adequacy of this warning because it did not make it clear that he had the right to have an attorney present throughout the interrogation.[347] The Supreme Court rejected that argument and concluded that the warning satisfied *Miranda*'s requirements:

> The Tampa officers did not entirely omit any information *Miranda* required them to impart. They informed Powell that he had the right to talk to a lawyer before answering any of their questions and the right to use any of his rights at any time he wanted during the interview. The first statement communicated that Powell could consult with a lawyer before answering any particular question, and the second statement confirmed that he could exercise that right while the interrogation was underway. In combination, the two warnings reasonably conveyed Powell's right to have an attorney present, not only at the outset of interrogation, but at all times.[348]

---

[344] *Id.* at 467.

[345] California v. Prysock, 453 U.S. 355, 359 (1981).

[346] Florida v. Powell, 559 U.S. 50, 54 (2010).

[347] *Id.*

[348] *Id.* at 62 (internal quotations and alternations omitted).

By contrast, warnings will be deemed invalid if one or more of the essential *Miranda* rights are omitted. For example, in *Watson v. Detella*, the court held that the warnings police gave were inadequate because they merely informed the suspect of a right to counsel without explaining a lawyer would be appointed to assist the suspect during interrogation if the suspect could not afford one for himself.[349] Similarly in *United States v. Tillman*, warnings were also determined to be inadequate because the suspect was not told that if he gave up his right to silence, whatever he said could be used against him.[350] To avoid such problems, most law enforcement agencies distribute *Miranda* warning cards for their officers to use when informing persons subjected to custodial interrogation of their rights.

B. Manner in Which Law Enforcement Administers Warnings

Miranda warnings must be stated clearly in a language understood by the suspect. Moreover, the warnings must be delivered in an unhurried manner so that suspects understand their rights and feel free to invoke them without fear. The warnings should not be given in a careless, indifferent, or superficial manner. When warnings are given to an immature, illiterate, or impaired person, the warnings must be administered in a manner that the person can comprehend and act upon intelligently. If necessary, the officer should explain and interpret the warnings. The test is whether the words used by the officer, in light of the age, intelligence, and demeanor of the person being interrogated, conveyed a clear understanding of all *Miranda* rights.[351]

C. Timing of Warnings

Miranda warnings must be given before beginning custodial interrogation in a language the suspect understands. But the passage of time can complicate matters.

---

[349] Watson v. Detella, 122 F.3d 450 (7th Cir. 1997).

[350] United States v. Tillman, 963 F.2d 137 (6th Cir. 1992).

[351] United States v. Rodriguez-Preciado, 399 F.3d 1118, 1127 (9th Cir. 2005).

1. Initial Interrogation

To comply with the mandate to give suspects their *Miranda* rights *before* they are subjected to custodial interrogation, police sometimes read *Miranda* rights upon taking the suspect into custody even though not required until someone is subjected to custodial interrogation. When this occurs, a significant amount of time might pass before custodial interrogation takes place. Although it is always a good idea to rewarn a suspect before starting any custodial interrogation, the passage of time usually does not compromise a *Miranda* warning. In fact, courts consistently uphold the integrity of *Miranda* warnings even when several hours have elapsed between the reading of the warning and the interrogation.[352] While the U.S. Supreme Court has not ruled on the upper limit of a permissible delay, lower courts have concluded that *Miranda* warnings go stale if suspects' understanding of their rights "erode to a point of insufficiency" with the passage of time.[353] Thus, one federal appeals court posited that a twenty-hour delay "seem[ed] to be at the upper end of the permissible range"[354] and a federal district court invalidated statements after an eighteen-hour delay.[355] By contrast, one federal appeals court upheld a delay of four days.[356] Longer delays appear to be impermissible absent other factors, such as suspects either being "summarily reminded" of their rights or expressly acknowledging awareness of their rights "immediately prior to the interrogation."[357]

---

[352] *See, e.g.*, United States v. Frankson, 83 F.3d 79, 83 (4th Cir. 1996) (two-and-a-half hours); United States *ex rel.* Henne v. Fike, 563 F.2d 809, 814 (7th Cir.1977) (nine hours), *cert. denied*, 434 U.S. 1072 (1978).

[353] United States v. Rouse, No. 4:09-CR-21-FL2, 2009 WL 2602347, at *8 (E.D.N.C. Aug. 21, 2009) (invalidating a thirteen-day delay between warnings and interrogation).

[354] United States v. Pruden, 398 F.3d 241, 247 (3rd Cir.2005).

[355] United States v. Jones, 147 F. Supp. 2d 752, 762 (E.D. Mich. 2001).

[356] *See, e.g.*, United States v. Webb, 311 F. App'x 582, 584 (4th Cir. 2009) (approving four-day period).

[357] *Rouse*, 2009 WL 2602347, at *9.

2. Subsequent Interrogations

Sometimes a suspect waives *Miranda* rights and submits to interrogation; then, after some time, police want to interrogate the suspect again. The general rule is that *Miranda* rights do not need to be repeated "so long as the circumstances attending any interruption or adjournment of the process [are] such that the suspect has not been deprived of the opportunity to make an informed and intelligent assessment of his interest involved in the interrogation, including his right to cut off questioning."[358] Determining when warnings have "gone stale," however, is not always easy.

In *Commonwealth v. Wideman*, the court listed five factors relevant to determining whether an accused must be reinformed of his or her *Miranda* rights:

- the time lapse between the last *Miranda* warnings and the accused's statement,
- interruptions in the continuity of the interrogation,
- whether there was a change of location between the place where the last *Miranda* warnings were given and the place where the accused's statement was made,
- whether the same officer who gave the warnings also conducted the interrogation resulting in the accused's statement, and
- whether the statement elicited during the complained-of interrogation differed significantly from other statements that had been preceded by *Miranda* warnings.[359]

Applying these factors, the *Wideman* court held that the *Miranda* warnings had "gone stale" because twelve hours had passed between the warnings and the time of interrogation, the defendant had been moved to another location, and a different set of police officers conducted the interrogation. But more recent cases have upheld statements made much longer than twelve hours after *Miranda* warnings were given under

[358] Bivins v. State, 642 N.E.2d 928, 939 (Ind. 1994).

[359] Commonwealth v. Wideman, 334 A.2d 594, 598 (Pa. 1975).

circumstances when other factors may have also contributed to the staleness of warnings.

Jones v. State, for example, upheld statements made two days after the warnings, even though "the interrogation was conducted by a different person (belonging to a different law enforcement agency)" in a different location and the statement "involved different events than earlier statements made immediately after *Miranda* warnings."[360] Key to the court's rationale was that there was "no reason to believe appellant suffered from any emotional state that would have impaired his understanding of the earlier-given warnings."[361] But *Ex parte J.D.H.*, invalidated a confession made sixteen days after *Miranda* warnings were given.[362] And in *State v. DeWeese*, the court invalidated a confession made seven days after the administration of warnings.[363] The *DeWeese* court used the same criteria listed nearly thirty years earlier by the *Wideman* court, but added an additional component: the "apparent intellectual and emotional state of the suspect."[364]

To avoid staleness problems, law enforcement officials should always readminister *Miranda* warnings whenever there has been a break in the continuity of interrogation.

---

360 Jones v. State, 119 S.W.3d 766, 800–01 (Tex. Ct. Crim. App. 2003).

361 United States v. Ferrer-Montoya, 483 F.3d 565, 569 (8th Cir. 2007).

362 *Ex parte* J.D.H., 797 So. 2d 1130 (Ala. 2001).

363 State v. DeWeese, 582 S.E.2d 786 (W. Va. 2003).

364 *Id.* at 799.

Chapter 8:

Multiple Interrogations

A. Attempts to Interrogate After an Unwarned Admission

In *Oregon v. Elstad*, a law enforcement officer investigating a burglary obtained an admission from the defendant in a custodial setting without first giving him the *Miranda* warnings.[365] Shortly thereafter, at the stationhouse, the defendant received complete *Miranda* warnings, waived his rights, and gave a written confession.[366] Because the defendant made incriminating statements while subjected to custodial interrogation before he received *Miranda* warnings, the courts consistently held that his prewarning statements were inadmissible.[367] The tougher question was the admissibility of the confession obtained at the police station after police gave *Miranda* warnings to the defendant.

The trial court had allowed the written confession into evidence over the defense's objection and the defendant was convicted. The Oregon Court of Appeals reversed the conviction, reasoning that it had been tainted by the initial violation of *Miranda*.

> Regardless of the absence of actual compulsion, the coercive impact of the unconstitutionally obtained statement remains, because in a defendant's mind it has sealed his fate. It is this impact that must be dissipated in order to make a subsequent confession admissible. In determining whether it has been dissipated, lapse of time, and change of

---

[365] Oregon v. Elstad, 470 U.S. 298, 300–01 (1985).

[366] *Id.* at 301.

[367] *Id.* at 302–03.

> place from the original surroundings are the most important considerations.[368]

The U.S. Supreme Court disagreed. The Court stressed that despite the *Miranda* violation before the officer obtained the first admission, no coercion or other illegal means were used to break the defendant's will. In other words, the first admission was voluntary. In admitting the written confession, the Court said:

> Because *Miranda* warnings may inhibit persons from giving information, this Court has determined that they need be administered only after the person is taken into "custody" or his freedom has otherwise been significantly restrained. Unfortunately, the task of defining "custody" is a slippery one, and "policemen investigating serious crimes [cannot realistically be expected to] make no errors whatsoever." If errors are made by law enforcement officers in administering the prophylactic *Miranda* procedures, they should not breed the same irremediable consequences as police infringement of the Fifth Amendment itself. It is an unwarranted extension of *Miranda* to hold that a simple failure to administer the warnings, unaccompanied by any actual coercion or other circumstances calculated to undermine the suspect's ability to exercise his free will, so taints the investigatory process that a subsequent voluntary and informed waiver is ineffective for some indeterminate period. Though *Miranda* requires that the unwarned admission must be suppressed, the admissibility of any subsequent statement should turn in these circumstances solely on whether it is knowingly and voluntarily made.[369]

Thus, the *Elstad* Court held as follows:

> We must conclude that, absent deliberately coercive or improper tactics in obtaining the initial statement, the mere fact that a suspect has made an unwarned admission does not warrant a presumption of compulsion. A subsequent administration of *Miranda* warnings to a suspect who has given a voluntary but unwarned statement ordinarily should suffice to remove the conditions that precluded admission of the earlier statement.

---

[368] *Id.* 303 (quoting State v. Elstad, 658 P.2d 552, 554 (Or. Ct. App. 1983), *rev'd*, 480 U.S. 298 (1985)).

[369] *Id.* at 309 (citing Miranda v. Arizona, 384 U.S. 436, 478 (1966), and quoting Michigan v. Tucker, 417 U.S. 433, 446 (1974)).

> In such circumstances, the finder of fact may reasonably conclude that the suspect made a rational and intelligent choice whether to waive or invoke his rights.[370]

In effect, *Elstad* significantly limited the application of the fruit of the poisonous tree doctrine to *Miranda* violations that did not occur as a result of "deliberately coercive or improper tactics."[371] The fruit of the poisonous tree doctrine applies only if the previous *Miranda* violation is accompanied by deliberately coercive or improper tactics in obtaining the initial statement. Without police misconduct during the initial interrogation, the initial *Miranda* violation will likely be deemed sufficiently attenuated by a voluntary waiver of a subsequent administration of *Miranda* rights.

The practical lesson of *Elstad* is that, after a voluntary admission is obtained as a result of the custodial interrogation of a suspect who did not receive *Miranda* warnings as a result of inadvertence, rather than intent to engage in some impermissible ploy, officers should carefully comply with all *Miranda* procedures in all subsequent interrogations before obtaining further statements, no matter how much time has elapsed between interrogations. This increases the chances subsequent statements may be admitted into evidence even if an earlier statement is ruled inadmissible because of a *Miranda* violation. Furthermore, even if an officer believes that a statement has been obtained in violation of *Miranda*, the officer need not warn that the statement cannot be used against the suspect. "Police officers are ill-equipped to pinch-hit for counsel, construing the murky and difficult questions of when 'custody' begins or whether a given unwarned statement will ultimately be held inadmissible."[372]

In the wake of the *Elstad* decision, some unscrupulous law enforcement officers developed a protocol to manipulate their way around *Miranda*. They would deliberately withhold *Miranda* warnings to obtain unwarned confessions; stop the interrogation for a break; return to the suspect; provide *Miranda* warnings; and then obtain a second confession

---

370 *Id.*

371 *Id.* at 314.

372 *Id.* at 316.

they thought would be admissible under *Elstad.* In *Missouri v. Seibert*, the U.S. Supreme Court ruled that *Elstad* did not cover such situations.[373]

The defendant's son in *Seibert*, who had cerebral palsy, died in his sleep. She feared that she would be charged with his neglect because he died with bedsores. So, she, her two teenage sons, and two of their friends decided to set fire to the home in the hopes of concealing the evidence. They left a teenager with mental illness in the home during the fire to make it seem as if the deceased son had not been left alone. That person died in the fire.[374] Five days later, police arrested the defendant. An officer deliberately interrogated her for more than half an hour without having administered *Miranda* warnings during which she confessed to having set the fire. After breaking for twenty minutes so that the arrested suspect could have coffee and a cigarette, the officer returned to the defendant, provided *Miranda* warnings, and then obtained a signed waiver of her rights.[375]

During her murder trial, Seibert sought to have both her prewarning and post warning statements excluded. During the suppression hearing, the officer "testified that he made a 'conscious decision' to withhold *Miranda* warnings, thus resorting to an interrogation technique he had been taught: question first, then give the warnings, and then repeat the question 'until I get the answer that she's already provided once.'"[376] Nonetheless, the trial court suppressed the unwarned statements under *Miranda*, but following the decision in *Oregon v. Elstad*, the court allowed into evidence the statements that Seibert made after she received *Miranda* warnings.[377] The U.S. Supreme Court ultimately reversed her conviction.

> By any objective measure, applied to circumstances exemplified here, it is likely that if the interrogators employ the technique of withholding warnings until after interrogation succeeds in eliciting a confession, the warnings will be ineffective in preparing the suspect for successive interrogation, close in time and similar in content. After all, the reason

---

373 Missouri v. Seibert, 542 U.S. 600 (2004).

374 *Id.* at 604.

375 *Id.* at 604–05.

376 *Id.* at 605–06.

377 *Id.* at 606.

> that question-first is catching on is as obvious as its manifest purpose, which is to get a confession the suspect would not make if he understood his rights at the outset; the sensible underlying assumption is that with one confession in hand before the warnings, the interrogator can count on getting its duplicate, with trifling additional trouble. Upon hearing warnings only in the aftermath of interrogation and just after making a confession, a suspect would hardly think he had a genuine right to remain silent, let alone persist in so believing once the police began to lead him over the same ground again. A more likely reaction on a suspect's part would be perplexity about the reason for discussing rights at that point, bewilderment being an unpromising frame of mind for knowledgeable decision. What is worse, telling a suspect that "anything you say can and will be used against you," without expressly excepting the statement just given, could lead to an entirely reasonable inference that what he has just said will be used, with subsequent silence being of no avail. Thus, when *Miranda* warnings are inserted in the midst of coordinated and continuing interrogation, they are likely to mislead and "depriv[e] a defendant of knowledge essential to his ability to understand the nature of his rights and the consequences of abandoning them. . . ." By the same token, it would ordinarily be unrealistic to treat two spates of integrated and proximately conducted questioning as independent interrogations subject to independent evaluation simply because *Miranda* warnings formally punctuate them in the middle.[378]

Siebert stands for the proposition that intentional attempts to circumvent *Miranda* by exploiting what is supposed to be a good-faith exception to *Miranda* rules under the type of narrow circumstances that occurred *Elstad* will result in suppression of both prewarning and post warning statements. In other words, law enforcement officers' intent matters in this context. Honest mistakes are the realm of *Elstad*, but calculated decisions to circumvent *Miranda* will result in suppression under *Seibert*.

---

[378] *Id.* at 613–14 (quoting Moran v. Burbine, 475 U.S. 412, 424 (1986)).

B. Attempts to Interrogate After Right to Silence Is Invoked

Recall that in the *Miranda* decision itself, the U.S. Supreme Court made it clear that once suspects have clearly and unambiguously invoked their rights, interrogations must stop.[379] Indeed, once a suspect clearly and unambiguously invokes the right to remain silent, police must "scrupulously honor[]" the defendant's assertion of the right.[380]

> [A]ny statement taken after the person invokes his privilege cannot be other than the product of compulsion, subtle or otherwise. Without the right to cut off questioning, the setting of in-custody interrogation operates on the individual to overcome free choice in producing a statement after the privilege has been once invoked.[381]

Nevertheless, under limited conditions, subsequent interrogation of a suspect who exercised the *Miranda* right of silence after being given warnings may be permissible.

In *Michigan v. Mosley*, police arrest the defendant in the afternoon in connection with certain robberies and a detective gave him the required *Miranda* warnings.[382] After indicating that he understood the warnings, the defendant declined to discuss the robberies, and the detective ceased the interrogation. Shortly after 6:00 P.M. the same day, a different detective had Mosley brought from a holding cell to the homicide bureau, administered another set of *Miranda* warnings, and then questioned Mosley about a murder that was unrelated to the robberies.[383] The defendant made an incriminating statement that was used against him at his trial. The Court held that admitting the defendant's statement into evidence did not violate *Miranda*. Even though *Miranda* states that the interrogation must cease when the person in custody indicates a desire to remain silent, *Mosley* reasoned that "neither this passage nor any other passage in the *Miranda* opinion can sensibly be read to create a *per se*

---

379 Miranda v. Arizona, 384 U.S. 436, 473–74 (1966).

380 *Id.* at 479.

381 *Id.* at 474.

382 Michigan v. Mosley, 423 U.S. 96, 97 (1975).

383 *Id.* at 98.

proscription of indefinite duration upon any further questioning by any police officer on any subject, once the person in custody has indicated a desire to remain silent."[384] The Court gave several reasons for allowing a second interrogation in *Mosley*. (1) Before the initial attempt to interrogate Mosley about the robbery, police complied fully with *Miranda*. (2) Once Mosley invoked his right to remain silent, police "scrupulously honored" his rights. The first detective ceased the interrogation when the defendant refused to answer and did not try to wear down his resistance by repeated efforts to make him change his mind. (3) The second interrogation was directed toward a different crime with a different time and place of occurrence. (4) The second interrogation began after a time lapse of more than two hours and only after the defendant had been given a fresh set of warnings. And (5) The second detective did not ask about any robberies, but rather exclusively focused on the unrelated homicide.[385]

Cases with fact patterns similar to *Mosley*'s routinely uphold the admissibility of incriminating statements made by a suspect after the passage of time.[386] These cases suggest the following guidelines for conducting a second custodial interrogation of a person who has exercised the *Miranda* right to remain silent:

- Scrupulously honor the person's right to terminate questioning at the initial interrogation.
- Allow a significant amount of time to intervene between the first and second interrogation attempts.
- Give the person complete *Miranda* warnings again.
- Do not employ any pressure to cooperate or other psychological ploys or tactics.

When all of these criteria are not satisfied, courts generally find that the logic of *Mosely* is not applicable and, accordingly, find that police violated *Miranda*. For instance, *United States v. Abdallah* determined

---

384 *Id.* at 102–03.

385 *Id.* at 104–05.

386 *See, e.g.*, United States v. DeMarce, 564 F.3d 989, 994–95 (8th Cir. 2009); Gore v. Sec'y for Dep't of Corr., 492 F.3d 1273, 1297–99 (11th Cir. 2007).

police violated the defendant's rights because an officer continued questioning the defendant after he said that he "wasn't going to say anything at all."[387] *Charles v. Smith*[388] held that police did honor the right to silence because they asked potentially incriminating questions just minutes after the defendant had invocated the right to silence. And *Perkins v. Herbert* determined that the invocation of the right to silence was not honored when officers failed to re-read *Miranda* rights to the defendant before they resumed questioning.[389]

C. Attempts to Interrogate After Right to Counsel Is Invoked

Miranda created a rigid rule that a suspect's request for an attorney is *per se* an invocation of Fifth Amendment rights, requiring that all interrogation cease. This rule is based on an attorney's unique ability to protect the Fifth Amendment rights of a client undergoing custodial interrogation.

1. The *Edwards* Rule

Once suspects indicate that they are not competent to deal with the authorities without legal advice, courts closely examine any later choice made without counsel's presence. Indeed, although an accused may waive *Miranda* rights and submit to interrogation, the U.S. Supreme Court has recognized that additional safeguards are necessary after an accused has clearly asserted the right to counsel and remains in custody for *Miranda* purposes. The leading case in this area is *Edwards v. Arizona*.[390]

The defendant in *Edwards* had been arrested for burglary, robbery, and murder.[391] He was taken into custody, brought to a police station, provided with his *Miranda* rights, said he understood them, and then voluntarily submitted to questioning.[392] During the interrogation, however,

---

387 United States v. Abdallah, 911 F.3d 201, 214–15 (4th Cir. 2018).

388 Charles v. Smith, 894 F.2d 718, 725–26 (5th Cir. 1990).

389 Perkins v. Herbert, 596 F.3d 161, 174 (2d Cir. 2010).

390 Edwards v. Arizona, 451 U.S. 477 (1981).

391 *Id.* at 478.

392 *Id.*

he eventually stated that he wanted an attorney.[393] "At that point, questioning ceased and Edwards was taken to county jail."[394]

The following morning, two detectives (not the police officers who had originally interrogated Edwards at the police station) arrived at the county jail to see Edwards. Edwards told a detention officer that he did not want to speak with the detectives who wanted to talk with him, but the jail guard told Edwards that "he had" to talk with them.[395]

> The officers identified themselves, stated they wanted to talk to him, and informed him of his *Miranda* rights. Edwards was willing to talk, but he first wanted to hear the taped statement of the alleged accomplice who had implicated him. After listening to the tape for several minutes, petitioner said that he would make a statement so long as it was not tape-recorded. The detectives informed him that the recording was irrelevant since they could testify in court concerning whatever he said. Edwards replied: "I'll tell you anything you want to know, but I don't want it on tape." He thereupon implicated himself in the crime.[396]

The U.S. Supreme Court ultimately held that incriminating statements Edwards made during his jailhouse conversation with the detectives violated Edwards' rights under the Fifth and Fourteenth Amendments:

> [W]hen an accused has invoked his right to have counsel present during custodial interrogation, a valid waiver of that right cannot be established by showing only that he responded to further police-initiated custodial interrogation even if he has been advised of his rights. We further hold that an accused, such as [the defendant], having expressed his desire to deal with the police only through counsel, is not subject to further interrogation by the authorities until counsel has been made available to him, unless the accused himself initiates further communication, exchanges, or conversations with the police.[397]

---

393 *Id.* at 479.

394 *Id.*

395 *Id.*

396 *Id.*

397 *Id.* at 484–85.

Edwards reinforced *Miranda*'s protections by superimposing a "second layer of prophylaxis" on safeguarding the right to counsel under *Miranda* for suspects who invoked their rights and remained in custody.[398]

> Under this rule, a voluntary *Miranda* waiver is sufficient at the time of an initial attempted interrogation to protect a suspect's right to have counsel present, but it is not sufficient at the time of subsequent attempts if the suspect initially requested the presence of counsel. The implicit assumption, of course, is that the subsequent requests for interrogation pose a significantly greater risk of coercion. That increased risk results not only from the police's persistence in trying to get the suspect to talk, but also from the continued pressure that begins when the individual is taken into custody as a suspect and sought to be interrogated—pressure likely to "increase as custody is prolonged . . . ." The *Edwards* presumption of involuntariness ensures that police will not take advantage of the mounting coercive pressures of "prolonged police custody," by repeatedly attempting to question a suspect who previously requested counsel until the suspect is "badgered into submission . . . ."[399]

Thus, under *Edwards*, once a suspect clearly invokes the right to counsel, "interrogation must cease, and officials may not reinitiate interrogation without counsel present, whether or not the accused has consulted with his attorney."[400]

2. Consultation with an Attorney versus the Presence of an Attorney

The *Edwards* rule has no time limitation and is effective as long as a suspect remains in *Miranda* custody. Therefore, once a defendant invokes the right to counsel, the police are barred from initiating further custodial interrogation of the defendant on the charges in question unless defense counsel is present at the interview. In other words, *Edwards*' rule barring law enforcement from seeking to reinitiate interrogation of a suspect in continuous custody does not end just because that suspect has consulted

---

[398] McNeil v. Wisconsin, 501 U.S. 171, 176 (1991).

[399] Maryland v. Shatzer, 559 U.S. 98, 105 (quoting Minnick v. Mississippi, 498 U.S. 146, 153 (1990); Arizona v. Roberson, 486 U.S. 675, 686 (1988); *id.* at 690 (Kennedy, J., dissenting)).

[400] *Minnick*, 498 U.S. at 153.

with an attorney. The U.S. Supreme Court explained why in *Minnick v. Mississippi*.[401]

Law enforcement in California arrested Minnick in that state while he was a fugitive on an outstanding warrant for murder in Mississippi. While he was being held in a San Diego jail, federal agents came to interview him. He refused, but was told by jail officials that he would "have to go down [to the interview] or else." The agents advised Minnick of his *Miranda* rights, he acknowledged that he understood them, and then he refused to sign a form waiving his rights.[402] He did, however, agree to answer a few questions. At one point, he terminated the interview and said, "Come back Monday when I have a lawyer" and indicated that when he had a lawyer present, he would make a more complete statement.[403] An appointed attorney subsequently spoke with Minnick two or three times.

A local sheriff's deputy subsequently came to interview Minnick. As with his first meeting with FBI agents, jail personnel told Minnick that he would "have to talk" with the deputy and "could not refuse."[404] Minnick therefore went and, as with the first interview, he received *Miranda* warnings and refused to sign a waiver of them. Yet, he spoke with the deputy and made incriminating statements that were used against him at trial. He appealed his conviction, arguing that the deputy's questioning of him violated *Edwards*. The Mississippi Supreme Court rejected that claim, reasoning that Edwards had been satisfied because questioning did not occur until after counsel had consulted with Minnick.[405] The U.S. Supreme Court reversed, quoting language from *Miranda* that "once individual in custody invokes his right to counsel, interrogation 'must cease until an attorney is present'; at that point, 'the individual must have an opportunity to confer with the attorney and to have him present during any subsequent questioning.'"[406]

---

401 *Id.* at 146.

402 *Id.* at 148.

403 *Id.* at 148–49.

404 *Id.* at 149.

405 *Id.* at 149–50 (citing Minnick v. State, 551 So. 2d 77, 83 (Miss. 1988), *rev'd*, 498 U.S. 146 (1990)).

406 *Id.* at 150 (quoting Miranda v. Arizona, 384 U.S. 436, 474 (1966)).

> A single consultation with an attorney does not remove the suspect from persistent attempts by officials to persuade him to waive his rights, or from the coercive pressures that accompany custody and that may increase as custody is prolonged. The case before us well illustrates the pressures, and abuses, that may be concomitants of custody. Petitioner testified that though he resisted, he was required to submit to both the FBI and the [sheriff's deputy] interviews. In the latter instance, the compulsion to submit to interrogation followed petitioner's unequivocal request during the FBI interview that questioning cease until counsel was present. The case illustrates also that consultation is not always effective in instructing the suspect of his rights. One plausible interpretation of the record is that petitioner thought he could keep his admissions out of evidence by refusing to sign a formal waiver of rights. If the authorities had complied with Minnick's request to have counsel present during interrogation, the attorney could have corrected Minnick's misunderstanding, or indeed counseled him that he need not make a statement at all. We decline to remove protection from police-initiated questioning based on isolated consultations with counsel who is absent when the interrogation resumes.[407]

3. The *Edwards* Rule is Not Offense-Specific

Edwards' prohibition on police-initiated interrogations after an invocation of the right to counsel does not just apply to the crime or crimes about which law enforcement first sought to question a suspect. Rather, the ban on further interrogation until counsel is present applies to all crimes for which the person might be suspected pursuant to the U.S. Supreme Court's ruling in *Arizona v. Roberson*.[408]

In *Roberson*, the defendant was arrested for a "just-completed" burglary and, after receiving *Miranda* warnings, stated that he "wanted a lawyer before answering any questions."[409] Three days later, while he was still in custody, a different officer subsequently interrogated him about a different burglary than the one for which he was arrested. During that interrogation, the defendant incriminated himself in the burglary that had

---

[407] *Id.* at 153–54.

[408] Arizona v. Roberson, 486 U.S. 675 (1988).

[409] *Id.* at 678.

prompted his arrest and the initial attempt at interrogating him.[410] In upholding the exclusion of those statements, the Court rejected the State of Arizona's argument that invocation of the right to counsel should be treated in the same way that *Michigan v. Mosley* treated invocation of the right to remain silent—namely that they be offense-specific:

> [Arizona] points to our holding in *Michigan v. Mosley* . . . that when a suspect asserts his right to cut off questioning, the police may "scrupulously honor" that right by "immediately ceasing the interrogation, resuming questioning only after the passage of a significant period of time and the provision of a fresh set of warnings, and restricting the second interrogation to a crime that had not been a subject of the earlier interrogation." The police in this case followed precisely that course, claims the State. However, as *Mosley* made clear, a suspect's decision to cut off questioning, unlike his request for counsel, does not raise the presumption that he is unable to proceed without a lawyer's advice. . . .[411]

4. *Edwards* Rule Ends with a Sufficient Break in *Miranda* Custody

Because *Edwards* is not a constitutional mandate, but rather a judicially-prescribed prophylactic rule, lower courts interpreted its presumption as terminating when there has been a sufficient break in custody.[412] The U.S. Supreme Court endorsed this approach in *Maryland v. Shatzer*.[413]

While the defendant in *Shatzer* was incarcerated on unrelated charges, a detective attempted to question him about allegations that Shatzer had sexually molested his son. The defendant invoked his right to have counsel present during questioning and the detective scrupulously honored that request by terminating the encounter. Shatzer was released back into the general prison population and the investigation was closed. Two and half years later, a different detective reopened the investigation and attempted

---

410 *Id.*

411 *Id.* at 683 (internal alteration omitted) (quoting Michigan v. Mosley, 423 U.S. 96, 106 (1975)).

412 Maryland v. Shatzer, 559 U.S. 98, 105 (2010) (internal citations omitted).

413 *Id.* at 107–17.

to question Shatzer, who was still incarcerated. This time, however, Shatzer waived his *Miranda* rights and made inculpatory statements. The U.S. Supreme Court upheld the admissibility of those statements,

> When, unlike what happened in [*Edwards*, *Minnick*, and *Roberson*], a suspect has been released from his pretrial custody and has returned to his normal life for some time before the later attempted interrogation, there is little reason to think that his change of heart regarding interrogation without counsel has been coerced. He has no longer been isolated. He has likely been able to seek advice from an attorney, family members, and friends. And he knows from his earlier experience that he need only demand counsel to bring the interrogation to a halt; and that investigative custody does not last indefinitely. In these circumstances, it is farfetched to think that a police officer's asking the suspect whether he would like to waive his *Miranda* rights will any more "wear down the accused, than did the first such request at the original attempted interrogation—which is of course not deemed coercive. His change of heart is less likely attributable to "badgering" than it is to the fact that further deliberation in familiar surroundings has caused him to believe (rightly or wrongly) that cooperating with the investigation is in his interest. Uncritical extension of *Edwards* to this situation would not significantly increase the number of genuinely coerced confessions excluded. The "justification for a conclusive presumption disappears when application of the presumption will not reach the correct result most of the time.[414]

With that reasoning in mind, the majority in *Shatzer* concluded that "[t]he only logical endpoint of *Edwards* disability is termination of *Miranda* custody and any of its lingering effects. Without that limitation—and barring some purely arbitrary time limit—every *Edwards* prohibition of custodial interrogation of a particular suspect would be eternal."[415]

Shatzer, however, remained in custody to serve out his prison term on the unrelated crime. Just as lower courts held the prisoners are not necessarily "in custody" for *Miranda* purposes without some change in their usual circumstances that indicates a new arrest or some coercion

---

[414] *Id.* at 107–08 (quoting Smith v. Illinois, 469 U.S. 91, 98 (1984) (per curiam); Coleman v. Thompson, 501 U.S. 722, 737 (1991)).

[415] *Id.* at 108–09.

related to the interrogation as explained in Parts V and VI, the Court in *Shatzer* concluded that, "[w]ithout minimizing the harsh realities of incarceration, we think lawful imprisonment imposed upon conviction of a crime does not create the coercive pressures identified in *Miranda*."[416]

> Interrogated suspects who have previously been convicted of crime live in prison. When they are released back into the general prison population, they return to their accustomed surroundings and daily routine—they regain the degree of control they had over their lives prior to the interrogation. Sentenced prisoners, in contrast to the *Miranda* paradigm, are not isolated with their accusers. They live among other inmates, guards, and workers, and often can receive visitors and communicate with people on the outside by mail or telephone.
>
> Their detention, moreover, is relatively disconnected from their prior unwillingness to cooperate in an investigation. The former interrogator has no power to increase the duration of incarceration, which was determined at sentencing. And even where the possibility of parole exists, the former interrogator has no apparent power to decrease the time served. This is in stark contrast to the circumstances faced by the defendants in *Edwards*, *Roberson*, and *Minnick*, whose continued detention as suspects rested with those controlling their interrogation, and who confronted the uncertainties of what final charges they would face, whether they would be convicted, and what sentence they would receive.[417]

Accordingly, Shatzer's return to the prison's general population to live for a two-and-a-half-year period constituted a break in custody for *Miranda* purposes. The Court noted, however, that the particular facts of the *Shatzer* case provided no real guidance to law enforcement about how long a break in custody needs to be to end the application of the rule in *Edwards*. The Court decided that two full weeks are necessary. A fourteen-day period "provides plenty of time for the suspect to get reacclimated to his normal life, to consult with friends and counsel, and to shake off any residual coercive effects of his prior custody."[418]

---

416 *Id.* at 113.

417 *Id.* at 113–14.

418 *Id.* at 110.

Without at least a fourteen-day break in *Miranda* custody as explained in *Shatzer*, the *Edwards/Minnick/Roberson* line of cases bars further police-initiated interrogation even about *unrelated charges* unless counsel is present. As the Court stated in *Roberson*, "the presumption raised by a suspect's request for counsel—that he considers himself unable to deal with the pressures of custodial interrogation without legal assistance—does not disappear simply because the police have approached the suspect, still in custody, still without counsel, about a separate investigation."[419] In summary, unless counsel is present, or unless the accused initiates further conversations, a waiver of *Miranda* rights after invocation of the right to counsel is presumed to be involuntary.

Of course, if police action after the suspect has invoked his or her right to counsel does not constitute interrogation or its functional equivalent, then *Miranda*, *Edwards*, *Minnick*, and *Roberson* do not apply. Recall from Chapter 6, for example, the case of *Arizona v. Mauro*,[420] in which spouses were permitted to speak with each other while an officer was in the room. The couple knew they were being recorded and that recording was used against the husband at his murder trial. Because those actions were held not to constitute the functional equivalent of interrogation, it is of no relevance that the husband had invoked his right to counsel.[421]

5. Invocations of *Edwards* for Discrete, Limited Purposes are Not Valid

Sometimes, suspects invoke their right to counsel for a narrow purpose while attempting to retain their rights for other purposes. Such actions typically suggest that suspects are impliedly waiving their *Miranda* rights with regard to other aspects of a case. These are referred to as **selective waivers** (or partial or qualified waivers). To be sure, suspects can waive some *Miranda* rights while retaining others, but that is easier said than done. For instance, police need to honor an invocation of the right to counsel for the specific purposes that suspects specify, but they do not need to honor the invocation of the right to counsel for other purposes. In

---

[419] Arizona v. Roberson, 486 U.S. 675, 683 (1988).

[420] Arizona v. Mauro, 481 U.S. 520 (1987).

[421] *Id.* at 529.

United States v. Ivy, for example, the defendant said that he would only answer questions on a specific topic once he had consulted with a lawyer. The officer did not terminate the interview, but rather said, "All right. Let's talk about something else."[422] The suspect subsequently made incriminating statements that were used against him at trial. A federal appeals court upheld the admissibility of those statements over the defendant's challenge to them under *Edwards*. The court reasoned that "Ivy expressed his unwillingness to answer questions about where he obtained materials to make a bomb, and [the interrogating officer] honored this request by moving to a different subject."[423]

A common limitation that suspects impose during interrogations is that they will not provide a written statement without the presence of counsel, but they are nonetheless willing to talk to the police. Such behavior seemingly demonstrates that suspects are ignorant about the fact that both oral and written statements can be used as evidence of their guilt. Even though *Miranda* warnings specifically tell people that anything they "say" can and will be used against them in court, some people nonetheless agree to make statements without counsel present, perhaps believing that their lawyers will sort things out later. Whatever their reasoning, courts generally hold that an invocation of counsel for the purpose of a written statement does not constitute an invocation of counsel for oral statements. The leading case in this regard is *Connecticut v. Barrett*.[424]

In *Barrett*, the police provided the defendant in that case with the required *Miranda* warnings before they began questioning him. He signed a form acknowledging that he read and understood his rights, and then told the officers that he would not give a written statement without his attorney being present, but that he had "no problem" talking with them about the incident.[425]

> It is undisputed that Barrett desired the presence of counsel before making a written statement. Had the police obtained such a statement without meeting the waiver standards of *Edwards*, it would clearly be

---

[422] United States v. Ivy, 929 F.2d 147, 152 (5th Cir. 1991).

[423] *Id.* at 153.

[424] Connecticut v. Barrett, 479 U.S. 523 (1987).

[425] *Id.* at 525.

> inadmissible. Barrett's limited requests for counsel, however, were accompanied by affirmative announcements of his willingness to speak with the authorities. The fact that officials took the opportunity provided by Barrett to obtain an oral confession is quite consistent with the Fifth Amendment. *Miranda* gives the defendant a right to choose between speech and silence, and Barrett chose to speak.[426]

Barrett illustrates the dangers for suspects of proceeding without the presence of counsel. A fair argument could be made that he did not understand that the oral statements he made incriminating himself (which were recorded) would be just as damaging as a signed written concession. But the Supreme Court ruled against that distinction:

> We also reject the contention that the distinction drawn by Barrett between oral and written statements indicates an understanding of the consequences so incomplete that we should deem his limited invocation of the right to counsel effective for all purposes. This suggestion ignores Barrett's testimony—and the finding of the trial court not questioned by the Connecticut Supreme Court—that respondent fully understood the *Miranda* warnings. These warnings, of course, made clear to Barrett that "[i]f you talk to any police officers, anything you say can and will be used against you in court." The fact that some might find Barrett's decision illogical is irrelevant, for we have never "embraced the theory that a defendant's ignorance of the full consequences of his decisions vitiates their voluntariness.[427]

In a concurring opinion, Justice Brennan remarked that the "odd juxtaposition [of] a willingness to talk and an unwillingness to have anything preserved militates against finding a knowing or intelligent waiver of the right to silence."[428] But he concurred with the majority that Barrett's own testimony "revealed that he understood that he had rights to remain silent and to have an attorney present, and that anything he said could be used against him; nevertheless, he chose to speak."[429] Without such testimony, it is unclear whether the Court would have found that

---

[426] *Id.* at 529.

[427] *Id.* at 530 (quoting Oregon v. Elstad, 470 U.S. 298, 316 (1985)).

[428] *Id.* at 533 (Brennan, J., concurring).

[429] *Id.*

Barrett had knowingly and intelligently waived his rights under *Miranda–Edwards*, but subsequent lower court decisions applying Barrett suggest the outcome would have been the same.[430]

6. *Edwards* Ends if the Suspect Reinitiates Conversation with a Valid Waiver

Suspects may change their minds after invoking their right to counsel and reinitiate conversation with law enforcement. But because there are reasons to be skeptical of such changes of heart while someone is in custody, law enforcement officers are well advised to ensure that there is proof of the "necessary fact that the accused, not the police, reopened the dialogue with the authorities."[431]

Waivers of rights under *Miranda–Edwards* are explored in the next section. For now, it bears mentioning that once the right to counsel has been invoked, it is essential that any subsequent waiver of that right be initiated by suspects themselves, as *McKinney v. Ludwick* illustrates.[432] In that case, the defendant invoked his right to counsel. The next morning, the defendant waved down the officer to ask about future proceedings of the case and demonstrated "a willingness and a desire for a generalized discussion about the investigation."[433] The officer initially refused to talk with the defendant, explaining that his invocation of the right to counsel the previous night prevented him from doing so. But the defendant "would not be deterred . . . . [He] then signed a written statement indicating that he had asked [the officer] to discuss his case."[434]

---

430 *See, e.g.*, United States v. Martin, 664 F.3d 684, 688–89 (7th Cir. 2011).

431 Edwards v. Arizona, 451 U.S. 477, 486 n.9 (1981).

432 McKinney v. Ludwick, 649 F.3d 484 (6th Cir. 2011).

433 Oregon v. Bradshaw, 462 U.S. 1039, 1045–46 (1983) (plurality opinion).

434 *McKinney*, 649 F.3d at 490.

Chapter 9:

Waiver of *Miranda* Rights

After *Miranda* warnings have been given to a person about to be subjected to custodial interrogation, and the person has had an opportunity to exercise the rights, "the individual may knowingly and intelligently waive these rights and agree to answer questions or make a statement. But unless and until such warnings and waiver are demonstrated by the prosecution at trial no evidence obtained as a result of interrogation can be used against him."[435] In the *Miranda* context, a waiver is a voluntary and intentional relinquishment of a known right. A valid waiver of *Miranda* rights means that a suspect has knowingly, intelligently, and voluntarily given up the right to silence or the right to counsel.

The dissenting justices in *Miranda* worried that requiring law enforcement officers to give warnings to suspects prior to interrogation would severely impact the ability of police to investigate and solve crimes because if suspects were aware of these rights, they would not voluntarily choose to waive them. Recall that many commentators, including police, prosecutors, politicians, scholars, and the media, echoed these concerns.[436] Most studies, however, report that even after police administer *Miranda* warnings, between 75% and 93% of all suspects waive their rights and agree to talk to the police at the start of interrogations.[437] Moreover, once interviews begin, few suspects who originally waived their *Miranda* rights

---

[435] Miranda v. Arizona, 384 U.S. 436, 478–79 (1966).

[436] Richard A. Leo, *supra* note 57, at 622.

[437] *Id.* at 659 (75%); *see also* Paul G. Cassell & Bret S. Hayman, *Police Interrogation in the 1990s: An Empirical Study of the Effects of* Miranda, 43 UCLA L. REV. 839 (1996); Anthony J. Domanico, Michael D. Cicchini & Lawrence T. White, *Overcoming* Miranda: *A Content Analysis of the* Miranda *Portion of Police Interrogations*, 49 IDAHO L. REV. 1, 2 (2012) (93%).

subsequently assert them, with studies placing the percentage of suspects who do so between 1.1% and 3.9%.[438] Psychological research suggests that innocent suspects waive their rights roughly 80% of the time, compared to guilty persons who waive their rights at the much lower rate of 36%.[439] This is likely a function of innocent people, who feel they "have nothing to hide or fear, naively believ[e] their innocence will ultimately set them free; as a result, they often submit to questioning."[440]

A. Express Versus Implied Waivers

Suspects can validly waive their *Miranda* rights expressly or impliedly.

1. Express Waivers

Express waivers occur when a suspect says, writes, or otherwise acknowledges that he or she is aware of his or her *Miranda* rights and voluntarily elects to give up those rights with knowledge of the consequences of doing so. To obtain an express waiver, after *Miranda* warnings have been administered, a law enforcement officer should ask the suspect whether he or she understands the rights that have been explained. The officer should then ask the suspect whether he or she wishes to talk without first consulting a lawyer or having a lawyer present during questioning. If the officer receives an affirmative answer to both questions, the officer should carefully record the exact language in which the answer was given, preserving it for possible future use in court. The officer may then proceed with the interrogation.

If possible, the officer should always try to obtain a written waiver of rights from the suspect before questioning, such as the one that appears in

---

[438] Leo, *supra* note 57, at 653 tbl.1 (1.1%); Cassell & Hayman, *supra* note 437, at 589 tbl.3 (3.9%).

[439] Cassell & Hayman, *supra* note 437, at 859; Richard A. Leo, *Inside the Interrogation Room*, 86 J. CRIM. L. & CRIMINOLOGY 266, 276 (1996); Paul Softley, *Police Interrogation: An Observational Study in Four Police Stations*, HOME OFF. RSCH UNIT REP. 28, at 29 (1980).

[440] Domanico et al., *supra* note 437, at 9 (citing Saul M. Kassin & Rebecca J. Norwick, *Why People Waive Their* Miranda *Rights: The Power of Innocence*, 28 LAW & HUM. BEHAV. 211, 212 (2004)).

Figure 1. A written waiver is almost always ruled by courts to be sufficient, presuming that the suspect is literate and there is no evidence of police coercion. If a suspect refuses to sign a waiver form but agrees to talk with police, such an oral waiver is valid, as previously described, albeit such a waiver is harder to prove in the absence of other evidence, such as an audio or video recording of the oral waiver.[441]

2. Implied Waivers

Law enforcement officers may not always be able to obtain express written or oral waivers of *Miranda* rights. *North Carolina v. Butler* held that express waivers are not required.[442] **Implied waivers** are valid if, under the totality of the circumstances, evidence shows that a suspect knew of his or her *Miranda* rights and then voluntarily waived them. Factors to be considered include:

- whether the defendant understood the rights at issue,
- the defendant's willingness to speak,
- whether the defendant expressed any desire to remain silent,
- whether the defendant's answers were in a narrative form rather than monosyllabic responses,
- whether there are any facts that cast doubt on the voluntariness of the waiver, and
- whether the defendant subsequently exercises *Miranda* rights.[443]

---

441 *See, e.g.*, United States v. Oliver, 630 F.3d 397, 410 (5th Cir. 2011).

442 North Carolina v. Butler, 441 U.S. 369 (1979).

443 *See, e.g.*, State v. Stephenson, 915 A.2d 327, 334 (Conn. Ct. App. 2007).

Figure 1: *Miranda* Waiver Form

Before we ask you any questions, you must understand your rights:

- You have the right to remain silent.
- Anything you say can and will be used against you in a court of law.
- You have the right to an attorney.
- If you cannot afford an attorney, one will be appointed for you before any questioning if you wish one.
- You can decide at any time from this moment on to terminate the interview and exercise these rights.
- Do you understand each of these rights I have explained to you? Having these rights in mind, do you wish to talk to us now?

I have read and understand fully each of my rights, and I am willing to answer questions and make a statement at this time. I do not want the advice of an attorney at this time. I understand and know what I am doing . No promises or threats have been made to me.

Signature:	*Date:*	*Time:*

Signature of Officer Advising of Rights	*Date:*	*Time:*

Witness Signature:	*Date:*	*Time:*

The following is a summary of some of the guiding principles courts utilize in examining whether a valid implied waiver of *Miranda* rights occurred.

a. Silence Is Not a Waiver

The *Miranda* opinion made it clear that "a valid waiver will not be presumed simply from the silence of the accused after warnings are given[;] . . . there must be an allegation and evidence which show that an accused was offered counsel but intelligently and understandably rejected the offer. Anything less is not a waiver."[444]

---

[444] Miranda v. Arizona, 384 U.S. 436, 475 (1966).

Recall that in *Berghuis v. Thompkins*, the U.S. Supreme Court reinforced its prior holdings that the voluntariness inquiry in the Fifth Amendment context is not concerned "with moral and psychological pressures to confess emanating from sources other than official coercion," such as one's religious beliefs.[445] The case also had another component to it.

Police administered *Miranda* warnings to Thompkins, the defendant in the case, and then interrogated him about a shooting in which a victim had died. At no point did Thompkins say that he wanted to remain silent, that he did not want to talk with the police, or that he wanted an attorney. Rather, he was most silent during an interrogation that lasted nearly three hours, giving only "a few limited verbal responses . . . such as "yeah," "no," or "I don't know . . . " or occasionally "nodding his head."[446] About two hours and forty-five minutes into the interview, however, an officer asked Thompkins, "[d]o you believe in God?"[447] At that point, Thompkins made eye contact with the officer, answered the question in the affirmative, and began to tear up.[448] He then answered "yes" to two more questions: "Do you pray to God?" and then, "[d]o you pray to God to forgive you for shooting that boy down?"[449]

In a five-to-four decision, the Court extended its holding in *Davis v. United States*, which held that suspects must clearly and unambiguously invoke the right to counsel, by similarly requiring a clear and unambiguous invocation of the right to remain silent. Applying that rule, the Court reasoned that Thompkins' silence during most of his interrogation did not unambiguously invoke his right to remain silent. Rather, he impliedly waived the privilege against self-incrimination when he knowingly and voluntarily made a statement to the police.

> An "implicit waiver" of the "right to remain silent" is sufficient to admit a suspect's statement into evidence. *Butler* made clear that a waiver of

---

445 Berghuis v. Thompkins, 560 U.S. 370, 387 (2010) (internal alterations omitted) (quoting Colorado v. Connelly, 479 U.S. 157, 170 (1986)).

446 *Id.* at 375–76.

447 *Id.* at 376.

448 *Id.*

449 *Id.*

> *Miranda* rights may be implied through "the defendant's silence, coupled with an understanding of his rights and a course of conduct indicating waiver."[450] The Court in *Butler* therefore "retreated" from the "language and tenor of the *Miranda* opinion," which "suggested that the Court would require that a waiver . . . be 'specifically made.'"

Three other Justices joined Justice Sotomayor's dissent in *Berghuis v. Thompkins*, which said that the majority decision meant that "a suspect who wishes to guard his right to remain silent against such a finding of 'waiver' must, counterintuitively, speak—and must do so with sufficient precision to satisfy a clear-statement rule that construes ambiguity in favor of the police."[451] She pointed out that "[t]he question whether a suspect has validly waived" the right to remain silent is "'entirely distinct' as a matter of law from whether [the suspect invoked that right."[452] And she went on to criticize the majority's reliance on *Davis*:

> Davis' clear-statement rule is also a poor fit for the right to silence. Advising a suspect that he has a "right to remain silent" is unlikely to convey that he must speak (and must do so in some particular fashion) to ensure the right will be protected. . . . "What in the world must an individual do to exercise his constitutional right to remain silent beyond actually, in fact, remaining silent?" By contrast, telling a suspect "he has the right to the presence of an attorney, and that if he cannot afford an attorney one will be appointed for him prior to any questioning if he so desires . . . " implies the need for speech to exercise that right. Davis' requirement that a suspect must "clearly reques[t] an attorney" to terminate questioning thus aligns with a suspect's likely understanding of the *Miranda* warnings in a way today's rule does not . . . . The Court suggests Thompkins could have employed the "simple, unambiguous" means of saying "he wanted to remain silent" or "did not want to talk with the police." But the *Miranda* warnings give no hint that a suspect should use those magic words, and there is little reason to believe

---

450 *Id.* at 384 (quoting Butler v. North Carolina, 441 U.S. 369, 373 (1979); Connecticut v. Barrett, 479 U.S. 523, 531–32 (1987) (Brennan, J., concurring in judgment)).

451 *Id.* at 391 (Sotomayor, J., dissenting).

452 *Id.* (quoting Smith v. Illinois, 469 U.S. 91, 98 (1984) (per curiam)).

police—who have ample incentives to avoid invocation—will provide such guidance.[453]

Justice Sotomayor's critique of the majority's logic in *Berghuis v. Thompkins* led some commentators to conclude that the words used in *Miranda* warnings are fatally outdated since "telling a suspect that he has the right to remain silent is no longer accurate."[454]

b. Words Indicating a Waiver

In contrast to silence, which cannot constitute a valid waiver after *Berghuis v. Thompkins*, comprehensible oral statements of one's understanding and willingness to speak are usually acceptable as a waiver of *Miranda* rights. Examples of valid waivers are a suspect saying,

- "I might as well tell you about it."[455]
- "I want to say some things."[456]
- "That means I ain't got to say nothing right now, 'til I talk to my lawyer [but] . . . I can talk to you if I want to."[457]

Moreover, if a suspect indicates the desire to invoke *Miranda* rights in the future, rather than in the present moment, such an invocation will not be valid. Thus, the court in *Thompson v. State* ruled that a suspect had impliedly waived his right to counsel under *Miranda* when he indicated his desire to talk to a lawyer at some time in the future, but agreed to answer questions by police first without a lawyer being present.[458]

c. Actions Indicating a Waiver

As in other communication contexts, gestures can be a meaningful substitute for words. Thus, courts have approved nonverbal waivers,

---

453 *Id.* (quoting Soffar v. Cockrell, 300 F.3d 588, 603 (5th Cir. 2002) (en banc) (DeMoss, J., dissenting) (additional internal citations and alterations omitted).

454 Michael D. Cicchini, *The New* Miranda *Warning*, 65 SMU L. REV. 911, 918 (2012).

455 United States v. Boykin, 398 F.2d 483, 484 (3d Cir. 1968).

456 United States v. Castro-Higuero, 473 F.3d 880, 886 (8th Cir. 2007).

457 State v. Murphy, 747 N.E.2d 765, 778 (Ohio 2001).

458 Thompson v. State, 235 So. 2d 354 (Fla. Dist. Ct. App. 1970).

including nods[459] and shrugs.[460] But even in the absence of a gesture that clearly communicates a waiver, courts look to how suspects behaved to determine their intent. For example, sometimes suspects will indicate their understanding of *Miranda* rights and then simply begin to make statements without any other verbal or nonverbal indication of a waiver. Most courts hold that, once the suspect has been informed of *Miranda* rights and indicates an understanding of those rights, choosing to speak without a lawyer present is sufficient evidence of a knowing and voluntary waiver of the rights.[461]

Defendants have argued that a number of other actions or behaviors constitute either an invocation of *Miranda* rights, or evidence that an implied waiver was not knowing, intelligent, and voluntary. Even though courts are supposed to presume a lack of waiver in the *Miranda* context, it is clear that courts often construe the actions of suspects as implied waivers, just as the majority did in *Berghuis v. Thompkins.*

For instance, a request to see or talk with someone other than an attorney is not an assertion of *Miranda* rights, although as previously explained, denials of such requests may have some bearing on the voluntariness of the statements. In *Watkins v. Callahan*, the court found a valid waiver of *Miranda* rights when the defendant indicated he was ready to make a statement after calling his family instead of calling an attorney.[462]

In *Fare v. Michael C.*, police took a sixteen-year-old into custody and sought to question him about a homicide.[463] The police read the juvenile his *Miranda* rights and the following dialogue then occurred:

> Q: Do you understand all of these rights as I have explained them to you?
>
> A: Yeah.

---

[459] Ragland v. Commonwealth, 191 S.W.3d 569 (Ky. 2006).

[460] State v. Brammeier, 464 P.2d 717 (Or. Ct. App. 1970).

[461] United States v. Cardwell, 433 F.3d 378, 389–90 (4th Cir. 2005).

[462] Watkins v. Callahan, 724 F.2d 1038 (1st Cir. 1984).

[463] Fare v. Michael C., 442 U.S. 707, 710 (1979).

Q: Okay, do you wish to give up your right to remain silent and talk to us about this murder?

A: What murder? I don't know about no murder.

Q: I'll explain to you which one it is if you want to talk to us about it.

A: Yeah, I might talk to you.

Q: Do you want to give up your right to have an attorney present here while we talk about it?

A: Can I have my probation officer here?

Q: Well I can't get a hold of your probation officer right now. You have the right to an attorney.

A: How I know you guys won't pull no police officer in and tell me he's an attorney?

Q: Huh?

A: [How I know you guys won't pull no police officer in and tell me he's an attorney?]

Q: Your probation officer is Mr. Christiansen?

A: Yeah.

Q: Well I'm not going to call Mr. Christiansen tonight. There's a good chance we can talk to him later, but I'm not going to call him right now. If you want to talk to us without an attorney present, you can. If you don't want to, you don't have to. But if you want to say something, you can, and if you don't want to say something you don't have to. That's your right. You understand that right?

A: Yeah.

Q: Okay, will you talk to us without an attorney present?

A: Yeah I want to talk to you.

The Supreme Court of California ruled that the juvenile's request for his probation officer was the functional equivalent of asking for an attorney because the "probation officer occupies a position as a trusted guardian figure in the minor's life that would make it normal for the minor to turn to the officer when apprehended by the police."[464] The U.S. Supreme Court reversed, ruling that the juvenile had waived his *Miranda* rights by speaking to the police even though he had been denied a request to speak to his probation officer. The Court specifically rejected the notion that a request to speak with someone other than an attorney, especially a probation officer, could trigger *Miranda*'s protections:

> A probation officer is not in the same posture with regard to either the accused or the system of justice as a whole. Often he is not trained in the law, and so is not in a position to advise the accused as to his legal rights. Neither is he a trained advocate, skilled in the representation of the interests of his client before both police and courts. He does not assume the power to act on behalf of his client by virtue of his status as adviser, nor are the communications of the accused to the probation officer shielded by the lawyer-client privilege.
>
> Moreover, the probation officer is the employee of the State which seeks to prosecute the alleged offender. He is a peace officer, and as such is allied, to a greater or lesser extent, with his fellow peace officers. He owes an obligation to the State, notwithstanding the obligation he may also owe the juvenile under his supervision. In most cases, the probation officer is duty bound to report wrongdoing by the juvenile when it comes to his attention, even if by communication from the juvenile himself. Indeed, when this case arose, the probation officer had the responsibility for filing the petition alleging wrongdoing by the juvenile and seeking to have him taken into the custody of the Juvenile Court.[465]

It is important to note that irrespective of the Court's holding in *Michael C.*, many states have placed restrictions on the custodial interrogation of juveniles in the absence of a parent, guardian, or other "interested adult."[466] Indeed, most states have enacted laws that require law enforcement to "immediately notify a parent or guardian" upon taking a minor into custody, although most of these laws do not address whether

---

[464] *Id.* at 718.

[465] *Id.* at 719–20.

[466] *See, e.g.*, Naomi E. S. Goldstein, Emily Haney-Caron, Marsha Levick & Danielle Whiteman, *Waving Good-Bye to Waiver: A Developmental Argument Against Youths' Waiver of* Miranda *Rights*, 21 N.Y.U. J. LEGIS. & PUB. POL'Y 1, 50 (2018).

the parent can physically accompany the youth during the interrogation.[467] However, either by statute or judicial decision, at least nine states require a parent, guardian, or other interested adult, such as an attorney, to be notified before a juvenile may be found to have validly waived *Miranda* rights.[468] It does not appear that the presence of someone other than an attorney, however, actually helps juveniles understand their rights and mitigate the coercive nature of custodial interrogations of juveniles largely because parents or guardians "may have divergent interests from their children, may not fully understand *Miranda* warnings themselves, and may themselves be overwhelmed by police pressures."[469]

As a matter of federal constitutional law, a request for counsel made by a suspect to a friend or relative is not the same as a request to the police.[470] Thus, in a case in which a suspect told his brother to post a bond for him and to get him a lawyer, the suspect's request to his brother did not operate as an exercise of his *Miranda* rights even though the police were aware of the request. Moreover, the suspect's subsequent statements to the police indicated that he had impliedly waived his *Miranda* rights.[471]

---

467 *Id.* at 51 (listing statutes).

468 *Id.* at 51–52 (citing COLO. REV. STAT. ANN. § 19-2-511; CONN. GEN. STAT. ANN. § 46b-137; MONT. CODE ANN. § 41-5-331; N.C. GEN. STAT. ANN. § 7B-2101; OKLA. STAT. ANN. tit. 10A, § 2-2-301; State v. Presha, 748 A.2d 1108, 1114 (N.J. 2000); *In re* B.M.B., 955 P.2d 1302, 1312–13 (Kan. 1998); Commonwealth v. A Juvenile, 449 N.E.2d 654, 657 (Mass. 1983); *In re* E.T.C., 449 A.2d 937, 940 (Vt. 1982)).

469 *Id.* at 52 (citing Thomas Grisso, *Juveniles' Capacities to Waive* Miranda *Rights: An Empirical Analysis*, 68 CALIF. L. REV. 1134, 1155 (1980); Thomas Grisso & Carolyn Pomicter, *Interrogation of Juveniles: An Empirical Study of Procedures, Safeguards, and Rights Waiver*, 1 LAW & HUM. BEHAV. 321, 340 (1997); Kenneth J. King, *Waiving Childhood Goodbye: How Juvenile Courts Fail to Protect Children from Unknowing, Unintelligent, and Involuntary Waivers of* Miranda *Rights*, 2006 WIS. L. REV. 431, 468 (2006); Jennifer L. Woolard, Hayley M.D. Cleary, Samantha A. S. Harvell & Rusan Chen, *Examining Adolescents' and their Parents' Conceptual & Practical Knowledge of Police Interrogation: A Family Dyad Approach*, 37 J. YOUTH & ADOLESCENCE 685, 695–96 (2008)).

470 Moran v. Burbine, 475 U.S. 412 (1986).

471 People v. Smith, 246 N.E.2d 689 (Ill. App. Ct. 1969).

d. Implied Waivers Through "Initiating" Further Communication

As previously mentioned, suspects may invoke their *Miranda* rights and then change their minds and reinitiate conversation with law enforcement. Under the U.S. Supreme Court's decision in *Oregon v. Bradshaw*, such actions may constitute an implied waiver of rights:

> [T]here are undoubtedly situations where a bare inquiry by either a defendant or by a police officer should not be held to "initiate" any conversation or dialogue. There are some inquiries, such as a request for a drink of water or a request to use a telephone, that are so routine that they cannot be fairly said to represent a desire on the part of an accused to open up a more generalized discussion relating directly or indirectly to the investigation. Such inquiries or statements, by either an accused or a police officer, relating to routine incidents of the custodial relationship, will not generally "initiate" a conversation in the sense in which that word was used in *Edwards.*[472]

But when a suspect initiates a conversation about substantive or procedural matters concerning the crime, *Bradshaw* considers such initiation to constitute a waiver of *Miranda* rights. *Bradshaw* involved a suspect who was in custody and had invoked the right to counsel, thereby triggering the protections of *Miranda–Edwards*. The suspect subsequently asked a police officer, "Well, what is going to happen to me now?" The Court ruled that the suspect's question "evinced a willingness and a desire for a generalized discussion about the investigation; it was not merely a necessary inquiry arising out of the incidents of the custodial relationship."[473] Accordingly, the incriminating statements that the suspect made throughout the discussion he had with the police officer were deemed admissible.

2. Selective Waivers

Recall from the earlier discussion of attempts to interrogate after suspects selectively invoke their rights that courts generally give little

---

[472] Oregon v. Bradshaw, 462 U.S. 1039, 1045 (1983).

[473] *Id.* at 1046.

weight to such invocation as illustrated by *Connecticut v. Barrett*.[474] Rather, courts view restrictive statements that do not align with subsequent actions as attempted selective waivers of rights, so long as a suspect understands that they do not have to talk to law enforcement authorities without the assistance of counsel. Thus, a suspect's attempt to carve out a partial exception to an otherwise knowing and voluntary waiver will usually be ineffective. *United States v. Frazier* is a typical example of this.[475] In *Frazier*, the defendant agreed to talk with police without an attorney being present, but he refused to allow police to take notes during the interrogation. Although this indicated that he may have misunderstood that his oral statements could, in fact, be used as evidence against him in court, the court upheld his waiver and allowed his oral statements to be used against him at trial. The same result has occurred when suspects agreed to talk but refused to have sessions recorded.[476]

There are, however, cases in which defendants can make selective waivers of their rights for some purposes while preserving their rights to silence and counsel for other purposes as illustrated by *State v. Jones*.[477] The defendant in *Jones*, who was a juvenile, and his attorney agreed to allow police to administer a polygraph test to the defendant. After the test was concluded, however, police interrogated the defendant without his lawyer being present with regard to the answers he provided during the polygraph examination even though the defendant requested consultation with his attorney. The court ruled that *Miranda* was violated because the selective waiver as to the polygraph examination did not extend to being an implied waiver for any subsequent interrogation, reasoning that "a defendant's voluntary waiver of rights in order to take a polygraph test [does not] automatically becomes a strategic point where the police, without affirmative notice to a defendant's counsel and under the rubric of

---

474 Connecticut v. Barrett, 479 U.S. 523 (1987).

475 United States v. Frazier, 476 F.2d 891 (D.C. Cir. 1973).

476 *E.g.*, State v. Bell, 745 S.W.2d 858 (Tenn. 1988).

477 State v. Jones, 607 S.E.2d 498 (W. Va. 2004).

a "post-test interview," may conduct an interrogation that would under any other circumstances be utterly unthinkable."[478]

B. The Requirements for Valid Waivers of *Miranda* Rights

Regardless of whether express or implied, *Miranda* made clear that any waiver must be "made voluntarily, knowingly and intelligently."[479] Courts begin their evaluation of purported waivers by presuming that a defendant did not waive his or her rights. The prosecution bears the burden of persuasion to prove, by a preponderance of the evidence, that the words and actions of the suspect evidenced a knowing, intelligent, and voluntary waiver of his or her *Miranda* rights.[480] As a rule, courts will not presume that suspects waived their *Miranda* rights just because they ultimately confessed. Therefore, when no written waiver or unambiguous oral waiver can be obtained, law enforcement officers should record all circumstances surrounding the attempt to obtain an implied waiver so that the prosecution will have evidence to prove that the waiver was voluntary, knowing, and intelligent.[481]

1. *Moran v. Burbine*'s Two-Prong Test for Waivers

Courts examine the totality of the circumstances surrounding the validity of an alleged waiver of *Miranda* rights by examining two distinct lines of inquiry that the U.S. Supreme Court outlined in *Moran v. Burbine*.[482]

> First, the relinquishment of the right must have been voluntary in the sense that it was the product of a free and deliberate choice rather than intimidation, coercion, or deception. Second, the waiver must have been made with a full awareness both of the nature of the right being abandoned and the consequences of the decision to abandon it. Only if

---

[478] *Id.* at 505. *But see* Lewis v. Miller, 220 F.3d 485, 489 (7th Cir. 2000) (holding that when a suspect requests an attorney only for a polygraph examination and not for other purposes, then subsequent discussions constitute a waiver of *Miranda* rights).

[479] Miranda v. Arizona, 384 U.S. 436, 475 (1966).

[480] Colorado v. Connelly, 479 U.S. 157 (1986).

[481] *Id.*

[482] Moran v. Burbine, 475 U.S. 412, 421 (1986).

> "the totality of the circumstances surrounding the interrogation" reveals both an uncoerced choice and the requisite level of comprehension may a court properly conclude that the *Miranda* rights have been waived.[483]

The prosecution bears the burden of persuasion to prove, by a preponderance of the evidence, that the words and actions of the suspect evidenced a knowing, intelligent, and voluntary waiver of his or her *Miranda* rights.[484] Therefore, when no written waiver or unambiguous oral waiver can be obtained, law enforcement officers should record all circumstances surrounding the attempt to obtain an implied waiver so that the prosecution will have evidence to prove that the waiver was voluntary, knowing, and intelligent.

a. ***Burbine*'s Voluntariness Prong**

This prong is exclusively concerned with the absence of police coercion as illustrated by *Colorado v. Connelly*.[485] Connelly, of his own accord and without any prompting, approached a police officer and said that he had murdered someone and wanted to talk to the police about it. The officer immediately advised Connelly of his *Miranda* rights. Connelly responded by saying that he understood his rights, but he wanted to talk about the murder anyway "because his conscience had been bothering him."[486] It turned out that Connelly was mentally ill, suffering from schizophrenia. During an actively psychotic phase, he went to the police to confess because auditory hallucinations that he believed to be "the voice of God" commanded him to do so.[487] Even though his severe mental illness made him feel compelled to confess, Connelly's waiver of *Miranda* rights was held to be voluntary because it was free of any governmental coercion.

When governmental coercion is at issue, most courts examine the voluntariness of a *Miranda* waiver by inquiring if the suspect's capacity for self-determination was critically impaired. Chapter 5 explored the concept of voluntariness in significant detail.

---

483 *Id.*

484 *Connelly*, 479 U.S. at 157.

485 *Id.*

486 *Id.* at 160.

487 *Id.* at 161.

b. *Burbine*'s Understanding Prong

Burbine's second requirement is that a waiver must be made with full awareness of both the right being abandoned and the consequences of the decision to abandon that right. Normally, this prong is satisfied by careful administration of the *Miranda* warnings to a suspect.

> The Constitution does not require that a criminal suspect know and understand every possible consequence of a waiver of the Fifth Amendment privilege. . . . The Fifth Amendment's guarantee is both simpler and more fundamental: A defendant may not be compelled to be a witness against himself in any respect. The *Miranda* warnings protect this privilege by insuring that a suspect knows that he may choose not to talk to law enforcement officers, to talk only with counsel present, or to discontinue talking at any time. The *Miranda* warnings ensure that a waiver of these rights is knowing and intelligent by requiring that the suspect be fully advised of this constitutional privilege, including the critical advice that whatever he chooses to say may be used as evidence against him.[488]

Courts commonly consider a range of factors when examining the validity of *Miranda* waivers under *Burbine*, the most common of which are discussed in the next section of this subpart.

2. Specific Factors Considered When Applying *Burbine*'s Test for Waivers

This section discusses the circumstances surrounding interrogations that courts frequently examine to determine if a *Miranda* waiver was knowing, intelligent, and voluntary. Keep in mind that the list of factors presented here is not exhaustive because courts must consider the totality of the circumstances surrounding an interrogation; thus, other factors may also be considered.

a. Competency of the Suspect

The inquiry as to whether a suspect has the requisite level of comprehension to validly waive *Miranda* rights is directed at the

---

[488] Colorado v. Spring, 479 U.S. 564, 574 (1987).

competency of the suspect. In determining competency to waive *Miranda* rights, courts examine the totality of the circumstances surrounding the waiver, with no single factor controlling.

Intelligence. No specific level of intelligence constitutes a minimum threshold for suspects to be considered competent to waive their *Miranda* rights. Thus, suspects with below-average IQs may be competent to waive their rights. *Smith v. Mullin*, for example, upheld a waiver by a defendant with the cognitive abilities of a twelve-year-old because he had prior experience with the criminal justice system and understood *Miranda* warnings.[489] But when law enforcement personnel are dealing with an impaired suspect whose cognitive abilities are low, they must take special care to ensure that the language they use is understood by the suspect. Thus, for instance, a federal appeals court invalided a waiver from a defendant with an IQ of only 65 (indicated clinical intellectual disability) who demonstrated he had a "very impaired ability to understand everyday interpersonal exchanges," and yet, police ignored special procedures for questioning a suspect of particularly low intelligence.[490]

Education. No specific level of education constitutes a minimum threshold for suspects to be considered competent to waive their *Miranda* rights. *United States v. Bautista-Avila* upheld a waiver by a defendant with a sixth-grade Mexican education because the officer read him his rights in Spanish and the defendant said that he understood his rights.[491] And *United States v. Rang* held that a twenty-five-year-old defendant with a learning disability and limited education was still capable of making a voluntary, knowing, and intelligent waiver of rights because he was familiar with

---

489 Smith v. Mullin, 379 F.3d 919, 933 (10th Cir. 2004); *see also* United States v. Robinson, 404 F.3d 850, 861 (4th Cir. 2005) (upholding waiver of a sixteen-year-with a lower-than-average IQ because the defendant was "street smart" and claimed understanding of *Miranda* rights).

490 United States v. Preston, 751 F.3d 1008, 1021 (9th Cir. 2014); *see also* Bies v. Sheldon, 775 F.3d 386, 402, 404 (6th Cir. 2014) (invalidating a waiver from a defendant with an IQ of 60 (below the lowest one-half percentile) who possessed the communication skills of a ten-year-old, and objectively exhibited behavior that detectives should have recognized as calling into question his capacity to waive rights knowingly and intelligently).

491 United States v. Bautista-Avila, 6 F.3d 1360 (9th Cir. 1993).

Miranda, followed the officer's questioning, and demonstrated the ability to "comprehend complex concepts and long-term consequences."[492]

Age. Suspects who may be too young to understand *Miranda* warnings pose special problems for the criminal justice system. Developmental psychology has demonstrated that reasoning and decision-making skills continue to develop throughout childhood and early adolescence.[493] Specifically, research shows that advantageous decision-making progressively develops into early adulthood, most specifically in complex situations involving risks in which direct feedback on possible gains and losses is provided.[494] In the context of waivers, research consistently indicates that most teenagers under the age of sixteen do not understand either the language of *Miranda* rights or some of the concepts underlying those rights, such as the role of defense counsel in criminal prosecutions.[495] For example, Thomas Grisso, a clinical psychologist and leading expert in juvenile's understanding of justice processes, reported that one-third of children "with few or no prior felony referrals believed that defense attorneys defend the interests of the innocent but not the guilty."[496] Despite

---

492 *See, e.g.*, United States v. Rang, 919 F.3d 113, 118 (1st Cir. 2019).

493 Kimberly Larson, I*mproving the "Kangaroo Courts": A Proposal for Reform in Evaluating Juveniles' Waiver of* Miranda, 48 VILL. L. REV. 629, 649 (2003).

494 Bernd Figner & Elke U. Weber, *Who Takes Risks When and Why? Determinants of Risk Taking*, 20 CURRENT DIRECTIONS IN PSYCH. SCI. 211 (2011).

495 *See, e.g.*, Marty Beyer, *Immaturity, Culpability, and Competency in Juveniles: A Study of 17 Cases*, 15 CRIM. JUST. 26 (2000); Barry C. Feld, *Juveniles' Competence to Exercise* Miranda *Rights: An Empirical Study of Policy and Practice*, 91 MINN. L. REV. 26 (2006); Naomi E. Sevin Goldstein, Lois Oberlander Condie, Rachel Kalbeitzer, Douglas Osman & Jessica L Geier, *Juvenile Offenders'* Miranda *Rights Comprehension and Self-Reported Likelihood of Offering False Confessions*, 10 ASSESSMENT 359 (2003); Thomas Grisso, *Juveniles' Capacities to Waive* Miranda *Rights: An Empirical Analysis*, 68 CALIF. L. REV. 1134 (1980); Grisso & Pomicter, *supra* note 469, at 337; Allison D. Redlich, Melissa Silverman & Hans Steiner, *Pre-Adjudicative and Adjudicative Competence in Juveniles and Young Adults*, 21 BEHAV. SCI. & L. 393 (2003); Richard Rogers, Lisa L. Hazelwood, Kenneth W. Sewell, Hayley L. Blackwood, Jill E. Rogstad & Kimberly S. Harrison, *Development and Initial Validation of the* Miranda *Vocabulary Scale*, 33 LAW & HUM. BEHAV. 381 (2009); Woolard et al., *supra* note 469, at 695–96.

496 THOMAS GRISSO, JUVENILES' WAIVER OF RIGHTS: LEGAL AND PSYCHOLOGICAL COMPETENCE 129 (1981).

these facts, courts routinely uphold waivers by teenagers between the ages of fourteen and eighteen.[497]

By contrast, courts often find that juveniles who are preteens or younger lack the intellectual development to make a knowing, intelligent, and voluntary waiver of *Miranda* rights.[498] Recall, however, that several states have laws that require a parent, guardian, or other interested adult, such as an attorney, to be notified before a juvenile may waive *Miranda* rights—even though the presence of an adult who is not an attorney is unlikely to be of meaningful assistance to a juvenile potentially being subjected to custodial interrogation.[499]

Familiarity with the Justice System. A complete lack of familiarity with the justice system certainly does not call into question a suspect's competency to invoke or waive *Miranda* rights. Nonetheless, courts usually find that suspects who have some prior experience in the justice system are less likely to be susceptible to mild forms of psychological tactics used by police to get suspects to confess.[500] Thus, in a close case, prior criminal justice experience weighs toward the validity of a waiver of *Miranda* rights. For example, *United States v. Palmer* held a waiver to be valid—even though the defendant was going through heroin withdrawal at the time of the interrogation—because the defendant had sixteen prior arrests.[501] And *Hardaway v. Young* upheld a waiver by a fourteen-year-old defendant because he had been arrested at least nineteen times in the past and appeared to understand his *Miranda* rights as a result of his prior experience with the justice system, despite his relative youth.[502] Keep in

---

[497] *See, e.g.*, Hall v. Thomas, 611 F.3d 1259, 1288–89 (11th Cir. 2010) (upholding waiver from fifteen-year-old because police read *Miranda* rights twice, did not subject the defendant to coercion, and otherwise remained calm during the interrogation).

[498] *See, e.g.*, Harris v. Bornhorst, 513 F.3d 503, 512 (6th Cir. 2008) (invaliding waiver from a twelve-year-old who was inexperienced with criminal process and physically separated from his mother during an intense interrogation).

[499] *See supra* notes 468–469 and accompanying text.

[500] *See, e.g.*, United States v. Jacques, 744 F.3d 804, 815 (1st Cir. 2014) (referring to the defendant was a "veteran of the criminal justice system" when upholding the validity of a signed waiver).

[501] United States v. Palmer, 203 F.3d 55 (1st Cir. 2000).

[502] Hardaway v. Young, 302 F.3d 757 (7th Cir. 2002).

mind, however, that even great familiarity with the criminal legal system does not excuse the requirement that law enforcement duly administer *Miranda* warnings before engaging in custodial interrogation.[503]

Physical and Mental Condition. In *Mincey v. Arizona*, the U.S. Supreme Court determined that a police officer violated *Miranda* by interrogating a hospitalized patient who had been seriously wounded.[504]

> It is hard to imagine a situation less conducive to the exercise of "a rational intellect and a free will" than Mincey's. He had been seriously wounded just a few hours earlier, and had arrived at the hospital "depressed almost to the point of coma," according to his attending physician. Although he had received some treatment, his condition at the time of [the] interrogation was still sufficiently serious that he was in the intensive care unit. He complained to [the detective] that the pain in his leg was "unbearable." He was evidently confused and unable to think clearly about either the events of that afternoon or the circumstances of his interrogation, since some of his written answers were on their face not entirely coherent. Finally, while Mincey was being questioned he was lying on his back on a hospital bed, encumbered by tubes, needles, and breathing apparatus. He was, in short, "at the complete mercy" of [the] [d]etective . . . , unable to escape or resist the thrust of [the] interrogation.[505]

Based on the forgoing part of *Mincey*, courts generally invalidate waivers by suspects who were drifting in and out of consciousness during an interrogation.[506] By contrast, courts often uphold waivers under many circumstances in which suspects were injured or in pain, so long as they were alert and responsive during questioning.[507] *Reinert v. Larkins*, for example, upheld the defendant's implied waiver even though the interrogation was taking place in an ambulance as the defendant was being taken to a hospital because he was "alert and coherent" during

---

[503] *See, e.g.*, United States v. Anderson, 929 F.2d 96, 99 (2d Cir. 1991) (holding that *Miranda* warnings were required even though the defendant had been arrested twelve prior times).

[504] Mincey v. Arizona, 437 U.S. 385, 399 (1978).

[505] *Id.* at 398–99.

[506] *See, e.g.*, United States v. Taylor, 745 F.3d 15, 25–26 (2d Cir. 2014).

[507] *See, e.g.*, United States v. Khalil, 214 F.3d 111, 121–22 (2d Cir. 2000).

questioning.[508] *United States v. Cristobal* upheld a waiver by a defendant suffering from postsurgical pain despite being on a narcotic painkiller because the medication did not affect his thinking.[509]

Courts similarly uphold waivers from sleep-deprived suspects, provided that law enforcement personnel did nothing to cause the sleep deprivation or other engaged in behaviors that call into question the voluntariness of statements. The court in *United States v. Carpentino*, for example, upheld a waiver from a defendant who had not slept most of the prior night and had not eaten the morning of the interrogation, largely because the police provided water to the suspect several times and there was no evidence that the defendant asked for and was denied the opportunity to eat or sleep.[510]

Drug or Alcohol Use. Although drugs or alcohol certainly impair cognitive functioning, suspects under the influence of drugs or alcohol may nonetheless validly waive their *Miranda* rights when they are not in a stupor. The critical question in such cases is the degree of impairment. If the suspect is functioning reasonably well, then courts usually uphold their waivers. For example, although the defendant was under the influence of drugs and alcohol at the time he was interrogated, a federal appeals court upheld his waiver in *United States v. Reynolds* because he was alert and able to answer questions asked of him directly and logically.[511] A court similarly upheld a waiver in *United States v. Walker* even though the defendant was vomiting during the interrogation due to heroin withdrawal because a doctor said the defendant was alert and "with the program."[512] By contrast, *United States v. Outland* held a waiver was not valid because the defendant had overdosed on heroin and had been drifting in and out of consciousness just two hours before the time of questioning).[513]

---

[508] Reinert v. Larkins, 379 F.3d 76 (3d Cir. 2004).

[509] United States v. Cristobal, 293 F.3d 134, 142 (4th Cir. 2002).

[510] United States v. Carpentino, 948 F.3d 10, 28 (1st Cir. 2020).

[511] United States v. Reynolds, 367 F.3d 294, 298–99 (5th Cir. 2004).

[512] United States v. Walker, 272 F.3d 407, 412–13 (7th Cir. 2001).

[513] United States v. Outland, 993 F.3d 1017, 1022–23 (7th Cir. 2021).

b. Explicitness of the Waiver

In *North Carolina v. Butler*, the U.S. Supreme Court stated that "[a]n express written or oral statement of waiver . . . is usually strong proof of the validity of that waiver."[514] Indeed, the more explicit a waiver is, the more likely it is to be valid. For example, *Wilcher v. Hargett* upheld a waiver even though the interrogation involved repeated questioning of the suspect over six days because the defendant received *Miranda* warnings and signed written waivers before each questioning period.[515] However, even a meticulously obtained written waiver cannot overcome other misconduct that calls into question the legitimacy of a waiver. For instance, *Hart v. Attorney General of Florida* invalidated a written waiver obtained after careful explanation of *Miranda* because the interrogating officer contradicted the written warnings by saying that signing the waiver form "honesty will not hurt you" in response to the defendant's questions regarding the benefits of having counsel present during the interrogation.[516] And *Gilliam v. Sealey* invalided a signed waiver and written confession because officers had threatened the defendant.[517]

Accordingly, providing warnings in English to non-English-speaking suspects, or to suspects whose knowledge of the English language is minimal, will not suffice. Thus, *Koh v. Ustich* determined a written waiver signed by a person who spoke Korean, but not English, was invalid because, despite the defendant's nodding, he did not understand the contents of the form due to the language barrier).[518] But if *Miranda* rights are translated into a language that a suspect can understand, even if the translation is imperfect due to misspellings or grammar errors, then a waiver of those rights is usually upheld.[519]

---

[514] North Carolina v. Butler, 441 U.S. 369, 373 (1979).

[515] Wilcher v. Hargett, 978 F.2d 872, 877 (5th Cir. 1992).

[516] Hart v. Att'y Gen. of Fla., 323 F.3d 884, 893–94 (11th Cir. 2003).

[517] Gilliam v. Sealey, 932 F.3d 216, 236–37 (4th Cir. 2019).

[518] Koh v. Ustich, 933 F.3d 836, 846 (7th Cir. 2019).

[519] *E.g.*, Thai v. Mapes, 412 F.3d 970 (8th Cir. 2005).

c. Failures to Disclose Information About the Interrogation

In *Colorado v. Spring*, the defendant contended that the failure of police to inform him of the potential subjects of an interrogation constituted the type of trickery and deception condemned in *Miranda*, and thereby rendered his waiver of *Miranda* rights invalid.[520] Specifically, he complained that he thought he had agreed to talk about firearms offenses, but police also questioned him about a murder. Citing *Burbine*, the Court rejected his arguments and held that a valid waiver does not require that police supply a suspect with all useful information to help calibrate his or her self-interest in deciding whether to speak: "[A] suspect's awareness of all the possible subjects of questioning in advance of interrogation is not relevant to determining whether the suspect voluntarily, knowingly, and intelligently waived his Fifth Amendment privilege."[521]

d. Failures to Disclose Outside Information and Events

Recall that in *Burbine*, police failed to let Moran know that his public defender had been trying to contact him. Although Moran otherwise made a voluntary waiver and confessed, he later challenged the validity of his waiver on the grounds that it was not "knowing" because he did not know that his lawyer had been trying to contact him. The U.S. Supreme Court rejected this claim, reasoning that "[e]vents occurring outside of the presence of the suspect and entirely unknown to him surely can have no bearing on the capacity to comprehend and knowingly relinquish a constitutional right. . . . We have never read the Constitution to require that the police supply a suspect with a flow of information to help him calibrate his self-interest in deciding whether to speak or stand by his rights."[522] Keep in mind, though, that many states have rejected the majority's approach in *Burbine* for the reasons outlined in the dissent in that case.[523]

---

[520] Colorado v. Spring, 479 U.S. 564, 569 (1987).

[521] *Id.* at 577.

[522] Moran v. Burbine, 475 U.S. 412, 422 (1986).

[523] *See, e.g.*, State v. Alexander, 347 So. 3d 608 (La. 2020); State v. McAdams, 193 So. 3d 824 (Fla. 2016); State v. Roache, 803 A.2d 572 (N.H. 2002); Commonwealth v.

C. Effect of *Miranda–Edwards* in Court

Despite *Dickerson v. United States* holding that *Miranda* warnings are constitutionally required, violations of *Miranda* rights produce few consequences compared to those that are normally triggered by other violations of constitutional criminal procedure rights.[524] Several of these anomalies have already been discussed, but they are reiterated here to emphasize the full scope of the ways in which the courts—and the U.S. Supreme Court in particular—have systematically whittled away at *Miranda*.

1. *Miranda* Violations Are Barred Only in Prosecution's Case-in-Chief

Statements taken in violation of *Miranda* are inadmissible in court as substantive evidence to prove the defendant's guilt. Such statements are permitted to be used at trial for impeachment purposes.[525] Similarly, a statement taken in violation of *Edwards v. Arizona* may be used to impeach a defendant's false or inconsistent testimony at trial, even though the same statement may not be used as substantive evidence.[526] Criminal justice professionals should not interpret these cases as opportunities to evade the requirements of *Miranda–Edwards*. An admission or confession obtained in compliance with those cases is much more valuable to the prosecution than an illegally obtained voluntary statement to be used only for impeachment or discovery of witnesses.

2. Fruit of the Poisonous Tree Doctrine Inapplicable

Under the common law, illegally obtained evidence did not affect its admissibility in court. The **exclusionary rule** changed that. It was first developed in 1914 in the case of *Weeks v. United States* and was limited

---

Mavredakis, 725 N.E.2d 169 (Mass. 2000); Dennis v. State, 990 P.2d 277 (Okla. 1999); People v. Bender, 551 N.W.2d 71 (Mich. 1996); People v. McCauley, 645 N.E.2d 923 (Ill. 1994); West v. Commonwealth, 887 S.W.2d 338 (Ky. 1994); State v. Simonsen, 878 P.2d 409 (Or. 1994); State v. Reed, 627 A.2d 630 (N.J. 1993); Bryan v. State, 571 A.2d 170 (Del. 1990); State v. Stoddard, 537 A.2d 446 (Conn. 1988).

[524] Dickerson v. United States, 530 U.S. 428 (2000).

[525] Oregon v. Hass, 420 U.S. 714 (1975); Harris v. New York, 401 U.S. 222 (1971).

[526] Michigan v. Harvey, 494 U.S. 344 (1990).

to a prohibition on the use of evidence illegally obtained by *federal* law enforcement officers.[527] It was not until the 1949 case of *Wolf v. Colorado* that the U.S. Supreme Court took its first step toward applying the exclusionary rule to the states by ruling that the Fourth Amendment applied to the states through the Due Process Clause of the Fourteenth Amendment.[528] *Wolf*, however, left enforcement of Fourth Amendment rights to the discretion of the individual states and did not specifically require the application of the exclusionary rule. That mandate did not come until the landmark decision of *Mapp v. Ohio.*[529] With *Mapp*, the exclusionary rule became the primary method to deter Fourth Amendment violations.

The exclusionary rule generally requires that any evidence obtained by police using methods that violate a person's Fourth, Fifth, or Sixth Amendment rights must be excluded from use in a criminal prosecution against that person. In addition, the U.S. Supreme Court has also invoked the exclusionary rule to protect certain due process rights that are not specifically contained in the Constitution. For example, a confession that has been coerced and is, therefore, involuntary is excluded from evidence because it is a violation of due process of law.

The exclusionary rule is not limited to evidence that is the direct product of illegal police behavior, such as a coerced confession or items seized during an illegal search. The rule also requires the exclusion of evidence *indirectly* obtained as a result of a constitutional violation. This type of evidence is sometimes called *derivative evidence* or *secondary evidence.*[530] The prohibition against using derivative evidence is often called the **fruit of the poisonous tree doctrine,** the "tree" being the initial constitutional violation and the "fruit" being the evidence obtained as a direct or indirect result of that violation.

Although the fruit of the poisonous tree doctrine was originally developed in applying the exclusionary rule to unconstitutional searches, it has been applied equally to evidence obtained as the indirect result of

---

[527] Weeks v. United States, 232 U.S. 383 (1914).

[528] Wolf v. Colorado, 338 U.S. 25 (1949).

[529] Mapp v. Ohio, 367 U.S. 643 (1961).

[530] Silverthorne Lumber Co. v. United States, 251 U.S. 385 (1920).

other constitutional violations. Thus, evidence is inadmissible if it is acquired directly or indirectly as a result of an illegal stop, illegal arrest, illegal identification procedure, or involuntary confession. In this way, the fruit of the poisonous tree doctrine may lead to the exclusion of additional evidence beyond the evidence obtained during the initial constitutional violation. The U.S. Supreme Court, however, has limited this doctrine in two important ways in the Fifth Amendment context.

First, the fruit of the poisonous tree doctrine does not apply to physical evidence derived from statements made in violation of *Miranda* pursuant to *United States v. Patane*.[531] Under *Michigan v. Tucker*, the same is true for testimonial evidence, as *Tucker* held that a *Miranda* violation that resulted in the discovery of a witness did not preclude the government from later calling that witness to testify at trial.[532] Note, however, that as with many of the Court's more restrictive interpretations of *Miranda*, some states have declined to follow *Patane* or *Tucker* on state law grounds.[533]

Second, recall that *Oregon v. Elstad* held that when suspects subject to custodial interrogation make incriminating statements without having been given their *Miranda* rights but subsequently repeat those incriminating statements after receiving *Miranda* warnings, the latter set of statements will usually not be excluded as fruit of the poisonous tree.[534] Rather, the post-warning statements are generally admissible so long as the initial, unwarned statements were not obtained involuntarily or as a result of a deliberate scheme, as previously discussed.[535]

3. Section 1983 Claims Barred for *Miranda* Violations

After the U.S. Civil War, Congress enacted a law that has long been codified in Title 42, Section 1983 of the U.S. Code, which is commonly cited at 42 U.S.C. § 1983. That law allows individual people to sue state actors and those acting under the authority of state law for civil rights

---

[531] United States v. Patane, 542 U.S. 630 (2004).

[532] Michigan v. Tucker, 417 U.S. 433 (1974).

[533] *E.g.*, Commonwealth v. Martin, 827 N.E.2d 198 (Mass. 2005); State v. Knapp, 700 N.W.2d 899 (Wis. 2005).

[534] Oregon v. Elstad, 470 U.S. 298 (1985).

[535] Missouri v. Seibert, 542 U.S. 600 (2004).

violations. In *Chavez v. Martinez*, police interrogated a suspect while he was in the hospital being treated for gunshot wounds he sustained during an altercation with a different law enforcement officer. [536] Even though the interrogation interrupted the suspect's medical care, the officer refused to stop the questioning of the suspect—over the objections of medical personnel—until the suspect admitted that he had pointed a gun at an officer. He eventually made such an admission. However, at no time during the interrogation had the suspect been given his *Miranda* rights. The suspect was never charged with a crime, but he subsequently sued the police under Section 1983 for several claims, including an alleged violation of his *Miranda* rights. A federal district court ruled in his favor that the police had violated his Fifth Amendment rights and a federal appeals court affirmed that decision. But the U.S. Supreme Court reversed it in a highly fractured, plurality opinion, holding that (1) coercive questioning, in and of itself, does not violate the Self-Incrimination Clause without some corresponding use of the suspect's unwarned statements in criminal case against;[537] and (2) without such use, there could be no grounds for Section 1983 liability for a Fifth Amendment violation strictly on the basis of a law enforcement officer's failure to give *Miranda* warnings before engaging in custodial interrogation.[538] The Court left open the question of whether a due process claim could be maintained for such actions.

In *Vega v. Tekoh*, the U.S. Supreme Court went even further by barring Section 1983 actions for *Miranda* violations even when the incriminating statements are subsequently used against a suspect in a criminal trial.[539] The Court reasoned that "a violation of *Miranda* does not necessarily constitute a violation of the Constitution, and therefore such a violation does not constitute 'the deprivation of [a] right . . . secured by the Constitution.'"[540] Moreover, the Court claimed,

---

[536] Chavez v. Martinez, 538 U.S. 760 (2003).

[537] *Id.* at 767.

[538] *Id.* at 772–73.

[539] Vega v. Tekoh, 142 S. Ct. 2095 (2022).

[540] *Id.* at 2106.

> *Miranda* rests on a pragmatic judgment about what is needed to stop the violation at trial of the Fifth Amendment right against compelled self-incrimination. That prophylactic purpose is served by the suppression at trial of statements obtained in violation of *Miranda* and by the application of that decision in other recognized contexts. Allowing the victim of a *Miranda* violation to sue a police officer for damages under § 1983 would have little additional deterrent value, and permitting such claims would cause many problems.[541]

As a result of *Chavez v. Martinez* and *Vega v. Tekoh*, the only remedy for suspects who are interrogated in violation of *Miranda* is to have their unwarned statements excluded as substantive evidence against them at trial during the prosecution's case-in-chief. Unlike with some other civil rights violations, no civil rights enforcement mechanisms allow people to sue police officers who failed to honor *Miranda* rights.

4. The Fifth Amendment in Court Beyond *Miranda*

Separate and apart from how *Miranda* protects the privilege against self-incrimination during custodial interrogations, the Fifth Amendment also has relevance in court. One of the most important protections the Fifth Amendment offers to those accused of crimes is the ability not to testify:

> The freedom of a defendant in a criminal trial to remain silent unless he chooses to speak in the unfettered exercise of his own will is guaranteed by the Fifth Amendment and made applicable to state criminal proceedings through the Fourteenth. . . . And the Constitution further guarantees that no adverse inferences are to be drawn from the exercise of that privilege.[542]

If defendants could be compelled to testify, that could put them in a position to incriminate themselves. So, they refuse to take the stand at trial and put the prosecution to its burden of proof beyond a reasonable doubt. That right, however, would ring hollow if the prosecution were allowed to argue to the jury that it should draw inferences against a defendant who does not testify. Accordingly, the U.S. Supreme Court held in *Carter v.*

---

[541] *Id.* at 2107.

[542] Carter v. Kentucky, 450 U.S. 288, 305 (1981) (quoting Malloy v. Hogan, 378 U.S. 1, 6 (1964), and citing Griffin v. California, 380 U.S. 609 (1965)).

Kentucky that judges must issue a "no-adverse-inference instruction" to protect the Fifth Amendment rights of non-testifying defendants at the guilt phase of their trial: "[A] state trial judge has the constitutional obligation, upon proper request, to minimize the danger that the jury will give evidentiary weight to a defendant's failure to testify."[543]

In *White v. Woodall*, the defendant pled guilty to the rape, kidnapping, and capital murder of a sixteen-year-old girl because of the overwhelming evidence of his guilt.[544] Because he did not contest his guilt, his trial consisted only of the penalty phase of his case during. The defense called character witnesses, but the defendant did not testify on his own behalf. He asked the court to instruct the jury that the fact he did not testify should not prejudice him in any way, but the judge denied that request, reasoning that although the Fifth Amendment requires a so-called "no-adverse-inference instruction" to protect a defendant who does not testify during the guilt phase of a trial, the Amendment does not extend to the penalty phase of a capital trial.[545] After being sentenced to death, he appealed and lost. But a federal district court sided with him when he petitioned for *habeas corpus*, reasoning that the judge's refusal to give a no-adverse-inference instruction violated the Fifth Amendment privilege against self-incrimination.[546] The U.S. Supreme Court ultimately ruled against him. But it did so on technical grounds concerning the scope of *habeas* review. Specifically, the Court reasoned because it had never held that a no-adverse-inference instruction is required during the penalty phase of a capital trial, it was not unreasonable for the state courts to have ruled that defendants waive the privilege against self-incrimination by pleading guilty.[547]

> [The Court's precedents] leave[] open the possibility that some inferences might permissibly be drawn from a defendant's penalty-phase

---

[543] *Id.* at 305.

[544] White v. Woodall, 572 U.S. 415, 417 (2014).

[545] *Id.* at 418.

[546] *Id.* at 418–19 (citing Woodall v. Simpson, No. CIV. A. 506CV-P216-R, 2009 WL 464939, at *1 (W.D. Ky. Feb. 24, 2009), *aff'd*, 685 F.3d 574 (6th Cir. 2012), *rev'd and remanded sub nom.*, White v. Woodall, 572 U.S. 415 (2014)).

[547] *Id.* at 420–22.

> silence. In *[Mitchell v. United States*], the District Judge had actually drawn from the defendant's silence an adverse inference about the drug quantity attributable to the defendant. . . . We held that this ran afoul of the defendant's "right to remain silent at sentencing. . . . " But we framed our holding narrowly, in terms implying that it was limited to inferences pertaining to the facts of the crime: "We decline to adopt an exception for the sentencing phase of a criminal case *with regard to factual determinations respecting the circumstances and details of the crime. . . .*" "The Government retains," we said, "the burden of proving facts relevant to the crime . . . and cannot enlist the defendant in this process at the expense of the self-incrimination privilege. . . ." And *Mitchell* included an express reservation of direct relevance here: "Whether silence bears upon the determination of a lack of remorse, or upon acceptance of responsibility . . . is a separate question. It is not before us, and we express no view on it."
>
> Mitchell's reservation is relevant here for two reasons. First, if *Mitchell* suggests that some actual inferences might be permissible at the penalty phase, it certainly cannot be read to require a blanket no-adverse-inference instruction at every penalty-phase trial. . . . This alone suffices to establish that the Kentucky Supreme Court's conclusion was not "objectively unreasonable."
>
> Second, regardless of the scope of respondent's proposed instruction, any inferences that could have been drawn from respondent's silence would arguably fall within the class of inferences as to which *Mitchell* leaves the door open. Respondent pleaded guilty to all of the charges he faced, including the applicable aggravating circumstances. Thus, Kentucky could not have shifted to respondent its "burden of proving facts relevant to the crime. . . ." Respondent's own admissions had already established every relevant fact on which Kentucky bore the burden of proof. There are reasonable arguments that the logic of *Mitchell* does not apply to such cases.[548]

As a result of *White v. Woodall*, the issue of whether the Fifth Amendment privilege against self-incrimination bars adverse inferences from being drawn from a defendant's silence at sentencing technically

---

[548] *Id.* at 422–23 (quoting Mitchell v. United States, 526 U.S. 314, 325, 327–28, 330 (1999)).

remains an open question. Nonetheless, the language strongly suggests the privilege will not normally extend to the sentencing phase of criminal proceedings if a defendant enters a guilty plea.

Chapter 10:

Interrogation and the Sixth Amendment

The Sixth Amendment to the U.S. Constitution provides that "[i]n all criminal prosecutions, the accused shall enjoy the right . . . to have the Assistance of Counsel for his defense." Recall from Chapter 3 that *Escobedo v. Illinois* tied the Sixth Amendment right to counsel to *pretrial* criminal proceedings once a suspect had become the focus of an investigation.[549] Although *Escobedo* was short-lived, its core holding—that the Sixth Amendment right to counsel has application at pretrial stages of criminal prosecutions—remains a vital principle in constitutional criminal procedure.

A. Attachment of Sixth Amendment Right to Counsel

The right to counsel under the Sixth Amendment differs from the right to counsel under *Miranda* which flows from the Fifth Amendment. The sole purpose of the right under *Miranda* is to ensure that a suspect's will is not overborne by coercive police interrogation tactics while the suspect is in custody. Thus, it exists to prevent compulsory self-incrimination only when a suspect is subject to custodial interrogation. In contrast, the Sixth Amendment is not concerned with compulsion in the self-incrimination context; rather, it protects those facing criminal adversarial proceedings in court. Thus, the Sixth Amendment right to counsel is triggered—or **attaches**—when formal criminal proceedings "have been initiated against [a suspect] him whether by way of formal charge, preliminary hearing, indictment, information, or arraignment."[550]

---

549 Escobedo v. Illinois, 378 U.S. 478 (1964).

550 Fellers v. United States, 540 U.S. 519, 523 (2004).

Table 3 shows the stages of criminal cases and whether the Sixth Amendment right to counsel attaches because the stage is considered to be a critical one. The first of the two lines that appear in boldface text shows that pre-indictment interrogations are not considered to be a "critical stage" and, therefore, are governed by the Fifth and Fourteenth Amendments vis-à-vis *Miranda*, not the Sixth Amendment. The second line, however, shows that once someone is under indictment or has otherwise been formally charged, the Sixth Amendment right to counsel attaches. As the remainder of Chapter 10 will make clear, the attachment of the Sixth Amendment right to counsel comes with legal consequences that are distinct from those under the Fifth Amendment and *Miranda*. Most notably, once the Sixth Amendment right to counsel attaches and is invoked or asserted, authorities may not engage in any conduct that is designed to elicit an incriminating response from the defendant without the presence or waiver of counsel.[551] This means that defendants may not be questioned without their lawyers being present unless a valid waiver of the Sixth Amendment right to counsel is first obtained. Recall that in *Moran v. Burbine*, the Court found no Fifth Amendment violation when the police failed to disclose to the suspect that his family had retained a lawyer for him and that the lawyer had been trying to reach the defendant. Had formal criminal proceedings begun, and thus the right to counsel under the Sixth Amendment attached, a constitutional violation would have occurred.[552]

---

[551] Brewer v. Williams, 430 U.S. 387 (1977).

[552] Patterson v. Illinois, 487 U.S. 285, 296 n.9 (1988).

Table 3: Stages of Criminal Cases		
Process/Proceeding	*Critical Stage*	*Extent of Right*
Arrest	No	No lawyer required
Initial appearance	Sometimes	Lawyer required if a critical stage[553]
Bail	Usually	Lawyer required if a critical stage[554]
Charging	No	No lawyer required
Preliminary hearing	Yes	Lawyer required[555]
Grand jury	No	No lawyer allowed
Arraignment	Yes	Lawyer required[556]
Interrogation (pre-indictment)	**No**	**Lawyer on request**[557]
Interrogation (post-indictment)	**Yes**	**Lawyer required**[558]
Lineup (pre-indictment)	No	No lawyer required[559]
Lineup (post-indictment)	Yes	Lawyer required[560]
Plea bargaining	Yes	Lawyer required[561]
Trial	Yes	Lawyer required[562]

553 Rothgery v. Gillespie Cnty., 554 U.S. 191 (2008).

554 McDonald v. City of Chicago, 561 U.S. 742 (2010).

555 Coleman v. Alabama, 399 U.S. 1 (1970).

556 Hamilton v. Alabama, 368 U.S. 52 (1961).

557 Miranda v. Arizona, 384 U.S. 436 (1966).

558 Massiah v. United States, 377 U.S. 201 (1964).

559 Kirby v. Illinois, 406 U.S. 682 (1972).

560 United States v. Wade, 388 U.S. 218 (1967).

561 Brady v. United States, 397 U.S. 742 (1970); Tollett v. Henderson, 411 U.S. 258 (1973); Missouri v. Frye, 566 U.S. 134 (2012).

562 Gideon v. Wainwright, 372 U.S. 335 (1963) (felonies); Argersinger v. Hamlin, 407 U.S. 25 (1972) (misdemeanors).

Table 3 (continued)		
Process/Proceeding	*Critical Stage*	*Extent of Right*
Sentencing	Yes	Lawyer required[563]
Probation revocation	No	Lawyer at court's discretion[564]
Parole revocation	No	Lawyer at board's discretion[565]
First appeal	Yes	Lawyer required[566]
Discretionary appeal	No	No lawyer required[567]

B. Fifth Amendment "Interrogation" Versus Sixth Amendment "Deliberate Elicitation

The Sixth Amendment right to counsel attaches under circumstances that are qualitatively different from those giving rise to a Fifth Amendment right to counsel. Thus, *Miranda*'s focus on custodial interrogation is inapplicable when examining Sixth Amendment rights. Rather, the Sixth Amendment bars the use of any statements made by a defendant in response to the actions of law enforcement that might *deliberately elicit an incriminating response*. Deliberate elicitation occurs when state officials create "a situation likely to induce . . . incriminating statements without the assistance of counsel . . . ."[568]

The deliberate elicitation standard is broader than the protections afforded suspects under the Fifth Amendment because it prohibits authorities from engaging in conduct that would not be considered "interrogation" or its functional equivalent under *Miranda*. Perhaps one of the most notable differences between the two amendments' approaches is that the Sixth Amendment bars the use of any secret investigatory techniques, whereas the Fifth Amendment does not. Consider the following leading cases.

---

[563] Mempa v. Rhay, 389 U.S. 128 (1967).

[564] Gagnon v. Scarpelli, 411 U.S. 778 (1973).

[565] Morrissey v. Brewer, 408 U.S. 471 (1972).

[566] Douglas v. California, 372 U.S. 353 (1963).

[567] Ross v. Moffitt, 417 U.S. 600 (1974).

[568] United States v. Henry, 447 U.S. 264, 274–75 (1980).

1. Deliberate Elicitation Violates Right to Counsel

Once the Sixth Amendment right to counsel attaches, the state must not do anything that deliberately or knowingly interferes with that right.

In *Massiah v. United States*, after the defendant was indicted, federal agents obtained incriminating statements from him in the absence of his counsel.[569] While the defendant was free on bail, his co-defendant, in cooperation with the federal agents, engaged the defendant in conversation in the presence of a hidden radio transmitter located in the co-defendant's car. Because the defendant was not in custody, no Fifth Amendment rights under *Miranda* were applicable; however, because he had already been indicted, the defendant's Sixth Amendment right to counsel had attached. The U.S. Supreme Court determined that the statements were inadmissible because the government violated the defendant's Sixth Amendment rights by using "his own incriminating words, which federal agents had deliberately elicited from him after he had been indicted and in the absence of his counsel."[570]

The Supreme Court affirmed the continuing validity of *Massiah* in *Brewer v. Williams*, a case often referred to as the "Christian Burial Speech" case.[571] The defendant, Williams, had been arrested, arraigned, and jailed in Davenport, Iowa, for abducting a ten-year-old girl in Des Moines, Iowa.[572] He needed to be transported by police from where he was captured in Davenport to Des Moines where his trial would take place. His lawyer in Davenport was denied permission to ride in the back seat of the police car with Williams during the 160-mile drive.[573] Accordingly, both that lawyer and the one who was representing Williams in Des Moines advised him not to make any statements during the trip. Pursuant to their instructions, "[a]t no time during the trip did Williams express a willingness to be interrogated in the absence of an attorney."[574] The police officers transporting Williams agreed not to question him during the trip.

---

569 Massiah v. United States, 377 U.S. 201 (1964).

570 *Id.* at 206.

571 Brewer v. Williams, 430 U.S. 387 (1977).

572 *Id.* at 390–91.

573 *Id.* at 391.

574 *Id.* at 392.

However, soon after the police began their trip with the defendant from Davenport to Des Moines, one officer engaged the defendant in "a wide-ranging conversation covering a variety of topics, including the subject of religion."[575] One of the officers then said the following to Williams, whom he addressed as "Reverend":

> "I want to give you something to think about while we're traveling down the road. . . . Number one, I want you to observe the weather conditions, it's raining, it's sleeting, it's freezing, driving is very treacherous, visibility is poor, it's going to be dark early this evening. They are predicting several inches of snow for tonight, and I feel that you yourself are the only person that knows where this little girl's body is, that you yourself have only been there once, and if you get a snow on top of it you yourself may be unable to find it. And, since we will be going right past the area on the way into Des Moines, I feel that we could stop and locate the body, that the parents of this little girl should be entitled to a Christian burial for the little girl who was snatched away from them on Christmas Eve and murdered. And I feel we should stop and locate it on the way in rather than waiting until morning and trying to come back out after a snow storm and possibly not being able to find it at all."
>
> Williams asked Detective Leaming why he thought their route to Des Moines would be taking them past the girl's body, and Leaming responded that he knew the body was in the area of Mitchellville a town they would be passing on the way to Des Moines. Leaming then stated: "I do not want you to answer me. I don't want to discuss it any further. Just think about it as we're riding down the road."
>
> As the car approached Grinnell, a town approximately 100 miles west of Davenport, Williams asked whether the police had found the victim's shoes. When Detective Leaming replied that he was unsure, Williams directed the officers to a service station where he said he had left the shoes; a search for them proved unsuccessful. As they continued towards Des Moines, Williams asked whether the police had found the blanket, and directed the officers to a rest area where he said he had disposed of the blanket. Nothing was found. The car continued towards Des Moines, and as it approached Mitchellville, Williams said that he

---

[575] *Id.*

> would show the officers where the body was. He then directed the police to the body of [the victim].[576]

Because Williams had already been arraigned, formal adversarial proceedings had commenced against him; he, therefore, had a Sixth Amendment right to have legal representation during the time in which he made incriminating statements in response to the officer's "Christian Burial Speech." The Court said that there could be no doubt that the officer "deliberately and designedly set out to elicit information from Williams just as surely as and perhaps more effectively than if he had formally interrogated him."[577] Thus, relying on *Massiah*, the Court ruled that Williams's statements were inadmissible because they had been obtained by police in violation of his Sixth Amendment right to counsel.[578]

United States v. Henry upheld the suppression of statements made by an indicted and imprisoned defendant to a paid, undisclosed government informant who was in the same cell block.[579] Although the informant did not question the defendant, the informant "stimulated" conversations with him and developed a relationship of trust and confidence with him.[580] As a result, the defendant made incriminating statements without the assistance of counsel.

> It is undisputed that Henry was unaware of [his fellow cell-block inmate's] role as a Government informant. The government argues that this Court should apply a less rigorous standard under the Sixth Amendment where the accused is prompted by an undisclosed undercover informant than where the accused is speaking in the hearing of persons he knows to be Government officers. That line of argument, however, seeks to infuse Fifth Amendment concerns against compelled self-incrimination into the Sixth Amendment protection of the right to the assistance of counsel. An accused speaking to a known Government agent is typically aware that his statements may be used against him. The

---

576 *Id.* at 392–94.

577 *Id.* at 399.

578 *Id.* at 401.

579 United States v. Henry, 447 U.S. 264 (1980).

580 *Id.* at 273.

> adversary positions at that stage are well established; the parties are then "arms' length" adversaries.
>
> When the accused is in the company of a fellow inmate who is acting by prearrangement as a Government agent, the same cannot be said. Conversation stimulated in such circumstances may elicit information that an accused would not intentionally reveal to persons known to be Government agents. Indeed, the *Massiah* Court noted that if the Sixth Amendment "is to have any efficacy, it must apply to indirect and surreptitious interrogations as well as those conducted in the jailhouse." The Court pointedly observed that *Massiah* was more seriously imposed upon because he did not know that his codefendant was a Government agent.[581]

Five years after the decision in *Henry*, the U.S. Supreme Court extended Henry's logic in *Maine v. Moulton*.[582] In that case, the Court held that even when a confrontation between an accused and a police agent is initiated by the accused, the government may not deliberately attempt to elicit information without counsel present. In *Moulton*, two co-defendants had been indicted on several theft-related offenses. During a meeting in which the two defendants met to discuss strategy for their upcoming trial, Moulton suggested that the two kill one of the state's witnesses against them. The co-defendant and his lawyer subsequently met with police and confessed to his participation in a series of thefts that included the charges for which he and Moulton had already been indicted, as well as other thefts. In exchange for a promise that no further charges would be brought against him, the defendant agreed to testify against Moulton and otherwise cooperate in the ongoing police investigation. As part of that agreement, the co-defendant allowed a recording device to be placed on his telephone line so that police could record a conversation that he had with Moulton. During several telephone conversations, the co-defendant got Moulton to make several incriminating statements. He also got Moulton to make incriminating statements during meetings between the two defendants while the co-defendant was wired with a recording device.[583]

---

581 *Id.* at 272–73.

582 Maine v. Moulton, 474 U.S. 159 (1985).

583 *Id.* at 162–63.

The state of Maine attempted to distinguish the actions of the police in *Moulton* from those of law enforcement in *Massiah* and *Henry* because in those cases, "the police set up the confrontation between the accused and a police agent at which incriminating statements were elicited."[584] In contrast, Moulton had initiated the recorded telephone conversations and had requested the in-person meeting in which another conversation was recorded. The U.S. Supreme Court rejected this distinction and held that the guarantee of the Sixth Amendment includes the government's affirmative obligation not to circumvent the protections afforded the accused people who invoke their rights to rely on counsel as a "medium" between the accused and the government. The Court continued:

> [T]he Sixth Amendment is not violated whenever—by luck or happenstance—the State obtains incriminating statements from the accused after the right to counsel has attached. . . . However, knowing exploitation by the State of an opportunity to confront the accused without counsel being present is as much a breach of the State's obligation not to circumvent the right to assistance of counsel as is the intentional creation of such an opportunity. Accordingly, the Sixth Amendment is violated when the State obtains incriminating statements by knowingly circumventing the accused's right to have counsel present in a confrontation between the accused and a state agent.[585]

In *Fellers v. United States*, the defendant had been indicted by a grand jury on charges related to the distribution of methamphetamine.[586] When police subsequently arrested him in his home, they told him that he had been charged with distributing methamphetamine.[587] In response, the defendant made incriminating statements. In holding that the police violated his Sixth Amendment right to counsel, the Court stated:

> [T]here is no question that the officers in this case "deliberately elicited" information from petitioner. Indeed, the officers, upon arriving at petitioner's house, informed him that their purpose in coming was to discuss his involvement in the distribution of methamphetamine and his

---

584 *Id.* at 174.

585 *Id.* at 176.

586 Fellers v. United States, 540 U.S. 519, 521 (2004).

587 *Id.*

> association with certain charged co-conspirators. Because the ensuing discussion took place after petitioner had been indicted, outside the presence of counsel, and in the absence of any waiver of petitioner's Sixth Amendment rights, the Court of Appeals erred in holding that the officers' actions did not violate the Sixth Amendment standards established in *Massiah* . . . and its progeny.[588]

2. Passive Receipt of Information Does Not Violate the Right to Counsel

The consistent outcomes in *Massiah*, *Brewer*, *Henry*, *Moulton*, and *Fellers* should make clear that the Sixth Amendment protections in the realm of interrogations are sometimes broader than those of *Miranda* and *Edwards* in the Fifth Amendment context. However, as the Court stressed in *Moulton*, "the Sixth Amendment is not violated whenever—by luck or happenstance—the State obtains incriminating statements from the accused after the right to counsel has attached . . . ."[589] Thus, for example, a defendant's Sixth Amendment rights are not violated when an informant voluntarily reports the defendant's incriminating statements to the police. "[T]he defendant must demonstrate that the police and their informant took some action, beyond merely listening, that was designed deliberately to elicit incriminating remarks."[590] Applying this rule, a federal appeals court *United States v. LaBare* ruled that a defendant's incriminating statements to a cellmate were admissible when the cellmate simply reported the statements to federal authorities under a general agreement to report what he might hear from other prisoners about violations of law, but was instructed not to directly question anyone.[591] "Where a jail-mate simply agrees to report whatever he learns about crimes from other inmates in general . . . , there is not enough to trigger *Massiah*."[592]

---

[588] *Id.* at 524–25.

[589] *Moulton*, 474 U.S. at 176.

[590] Kuhlmann v. Wilson, 477 U.S. 436, 459 (1986).

[591] United States v. LaBare, 191 F.3d 60 (1st Cir. 1999).

[592] *Id.* at 65–66.

3. Offense-Specific Nature of the Sixth Amendment Right to Counsel

The Sixth Amendment right to counsel, unlike the right to counsel under *Miranda–Edwards* flowing from the Fifth Amendment's privilege against self-incrimination, is *offense specific*. Thus, invocation of the Sixth Amendment right to counsel bars police from deliberately eliciting incriminating information regarding only the offense at issue; it does not bar police-initiated interrogation or other activities designed to elicit an incriminating response on unrelated charges. The U.S. Supreme Court explained the logic of this approach in *McNeil v. Wisconsin*:

> The purpose of the Sixth Amendment counsel guarantee—and hence the purpose of invoking it—is to "protec[t] the unaided layman at critical confrontations" with his "expert adversary," the government, after "the adverse positions of government and defendant have solidified" with respect to a particular alleged crime. . . . The purpose of the *Miranda–Edwards* guarantee, on the other hand—and hence the purpose of invoking it—is to protect a quite different interest: the suspect's "desire to deal with the police only through counsel . . . ." This is in one respect narrower than the interest protected by the Sixth Amendment guarantee (because it relates only to custodial interrogation) and in another respect broader (because it relates to interrogation regarding any suspected crime and attaches whether or not the "adversarial relationship" produced by a pending prosecution has yet arisen).[593]

The prohibition against deliberate attempts to elicit information in the absence of counsel is not intended to hamper police investigation of crimes other than the crime for which adversary proceedings have already commenced. The police need to investigate crimes for which formal charges have already been filed as well as new or additional crimes. Either type of investigation may require surveillance of persons already indicted. Moreover, police who are investigating a person suspected of committing one crime and formally charged with having committed another crime may seek to discover evidence of either crime. In seeking evidence relating to pending charges, however, police investigators are limited by the Sixth

---

[593] McNeil v. Wisconsin, 501 U.S. 171, 177–78 (1991).

Amendment rights of the accused. Therefore, incriminating statements relating to pending charges will be inadmissible at the trial of those charges—even though police were also investigating other crimes—if, in obtaining the evidence, the government violated the Sixth Amendment by knowingly circumventing the accused's right to the assistance of counsel. On the other hand, evidence relating to charges to which the Sixth Amendment right to counsel had not attached at the time the evidence was obtained will not be inadmissible merely because other charges were pending at the time.[594]

In *Texas v. Cobb*, the defendant confessed to a home burglary but denied any knowledge about a woman and child's disappearance from the home.[595] He was indicted for the burglary, and counsel was appointed to represent him on that charge. He later confessed to his father that he had killed the woman and child in the course of the burglary, and his father contacted the police.[596] After police arrested Cobb and administered *Miranda* warnings, he waived his *Miranda* rights and confessed to the murders. On appeal of his capital murder conviction, he argued that his confession should have been suppressed because it was obtained in violation of his Sixth Amendment right to counsel. He claimed that the right attached when counsel was appointed in the burglary case, which was "factually related" to the capital murder charge. The U.S. Supreme Court rejected the claim and held that, because burglary and capital murder are not the *same offense* under Texas law, and because the Sixth Amendment right to counsel is "offense specific," the failure to obtain the defendant's counsel's permission did not bar the police from interrogating him regarding the murders. His confession was therefore admissible.[597]

C. Waiver of Sixth Amendment Right to Counsel

As with the Fifth Amendment right to counsel under *Miranda*, a defendant may waive his or her right to counsel under the Sixth Amendment. Also, as it is with the Fifth Amendment, there is a strong

---

594 Maine v. Moulton, 474 U.S. 159 (1985).

595 Texas v. Cobb, 532 U.S. 162, 165 (2001).

596 *Id.*

597 *Id.* at 173.

presumption against implied waivers of counsel in the Sixth Amendment context, given the essential function that defense counsel plays in the administration of justice. As the U.S. Supreme Court said in *Brewer v. Williams*,

> [it is] incumbent upon the State to prove "an intentional relinquishment or abandonment of a known right or privilege." That standard has been reiterated in many cases. We have said that the right to counsel does not depend upon a request by the defendant . . . , and that courts indulge in every reasonable presumption against waiver. This strict standard applies equally to an alleged waiver of the right to counsel whether at trial or at a critical stage of pretrial proceedings.[598]

Thus, to show that a valid waiver of counsel for Sixth Amendment purposes exists, the prosecution must prove the following two facts:

1. the defendant was aware of the right to counsel; and
2. the defendant knowingly, intelligently, and voluntarily relinquished the right.

This is qualitatively no different from waivers in the Fifth Amendment context under *Miranda*.[599]

1. *Miranda* Warnings Sufficient to Provide Knowledge of Right to Counsel

As previously explained, *Miranda* warnings were created by the U.S. Supreme Court to safeguard the Fifth Amendment privilege against self-incrimination. Despite this, *Patterson v. Illinois* held that the *Miranda* warnings are also sufficient to inform a defendant of the right to have counsel present during questioning once the Sixth Amendment right to counsel has attached, as well as the consequences of a decision to waive the Sixth Amendment right during such questioning:

> [W]hatever warnings suffice for *Miranda*'s purposes will also be sufficient in the context of post-indictment questioning. The State's decision to take an additional step and commence formal adversarial

---

[598] Brewer v. Williams, 430 U.S. 387, 404 (1977) (internal citations omitted).

[599] Patterson v. Illinois, 487 U.S. 285 (1988).

> proceedings against the accused does not substantially increase the value of counsel to the accused at questioning, or expand the limited purpose that an attorney serves when the accused is questioned by authorities. With respect to this inquiry, we do not discern a substantial difference between the usefulness of a lawyer to a suspect during custodial interrogation, and his value to an accused at post-indictment questioning.[600]

Thus, once a defendant suspect has been informed of his right to counsel under the Sixth Amendment by having been "admonished with the warnings prescribed by [the Supreme] Court in *Miranda*" and has been sufficiently apprised of the nature and consequences of abandoning his or her Sixth Amendment rights, the defendant's "waiver on this basis will be considered a knowing and intelligent one."[601]

2. Subsequent Waiver After Initial Invocation of the Sixth Amendment Rights

Recall that under *Edwards v. Arizona*, after a knowing and voluntary waiver of *Miranda* rights, law enforcement officers may continue questioning until and unless the suspect clearly requests an attorney.[602] Similar to the rule in *Edwards* for Fifth Amendment purposes, the U.S. Supreme Court has held that once a defendant has unambiguously invoked his or her right to counsel under the Sixth Amendment at or after the initiation of adversary judicial proceedings, any further interrogation of the defendant without counsel actually being present is not permitted if the police initiate the discussion.[603] But, as in the Fifth Amendment context invoking the right is important as illustrated by *Montejo v. Louisiana*.[604]

At a preliminary hearing required by Louisiana law, Montejo was charged with first-degree murder. Although he remained silent at the hearing, the court declared Montejo indigent and automatically appointed counsel to represent him. Later that day, the police approached Montejo

---

600 *Id.* at 298–99.

601 *Id.* at 296.

602 Edwards v. Arizona, 451 U.S. 477 (1981).

603 Montejo v. Louisiana, 556 U.S. 778 (2009).

604 *Id.*

and read him *Miranda* rights, after which he agreed to go along on a trip to locate the murder weapon.[605] During the excursion, he wrote an inculpatory letter of apology to the victim's widow.[606] Upon returning, Montejo finally met his court-appointed attorney. At trial, his letter was admitted over defense objection, and he was convicted and sentenced to death.

The state high court rejected Montejo's claim that the letter should have been suppressed under the rule of *Michigan v. Jackson*.[607] In *Jackson*, several defendants requested counsel at their arraignments on murder charges. Before counsel had been provided to them, police officers questioned the defendants after advising them of their *Miranda* rights. The defendants waived their *Miranda* rights and agreed to talk with police who, in turn, were able to obtain confessions from the defendants. The U.S. Supreme Court held that the confessions were obtained in violation of the Sixth Amendment right to counsel because police had initiated contact with the defendants after they had invoked their right to counsel and, in so doing, sought a waiver of that right before counsel had actually been provided to the defendants. The Louisiana Supreme Court reasoned *Jackson* did not apply because Montejo stood mute at his hearing while the judge ordered the appointment of counsel. Thus, he never actually asserted his Sixth Amendment right to counsel.

The U.S. Supreme Court upheld Montejo's conviction, but disagreed with the state court's rationale, believing its interpretation of *Jackson* would lead to practical problems because in roughly half the states counsel is appointed without a request from the defendant upon a finding of indigency. The Court also rejected Montejo's proposal that defendants should not have invoked their Sixth Amendment rights because such an approach would depart fundamentally from the rationale of *Jackson*, whose presumption was created by analogy to *Edwards*'s approach to protecting *Miranda* rights. Ultimately, the Court overruled *Jackson* and declared a new rule to protect criminal defendants' Sixth Amendment rights to counsel that mirrors *Edwards*'s anti-badgering approach in the

---

605 *Id.* at 781–82.

606 *Id.* at 782.

607 Michigan v. Jackson, 475 U.S. 625 (1986).

Fifth Amendment context—namely, that a defendant in custody cannot be interrogated once he has asserted his Sixth Amendment right to counsel unless the defendant initiates further communications with police:

> When a court appoints counsel for an indigent defendant in the absence of any request on his part, there is no basis for a presumption that any subsequent waiver of the right to counsel will be involuntary. There is no "initial election" to exercise the right that must be preserved through a prophylactic rule against later waivers. No reason exists to assume that a defendant like Montejo, who has done nothing at all to express his intentions with respect to his Sixth Amendment rights, would not be perfectly amenable to speaking with the police without having counsel present. And no reason exists to prohibit the police from inquiring. *Edwards* and *Jackson* are meant to prevent police from badgering defendants into changing their minds about their rights, but a defendant who never asked for counsel has not yet made up his mind in the first instance.[608]

The Court remanded the case to give Montejo an opportunity to argue that his letter of apology should still have been suppressed under the rule of *Edwards*. Thus, if Montejo clearly asserted the right to counsel when the officers approached him about accompanying them on the excursion for the murder weapon, then no interrogation should have taken place unless Montejo initiated it. On remand, however, relying on state law, the Supreme Court of Louisiana refused to consider whether Montejo had invoked his right to counsel under *Edwards* and therefore affirmed his conviction and death sentence.[609]

In light of *Montejo*, if a defendant reinitiates contact with police after requesting that counsel be provided under the Sixth Amendment (i.e., after asserting the right once formal criminal proceedings have been commenced against the suspect), and the defendant is readvised of his or her *Miranda* rights and then knowingly and voluntarily waives them, following the parallel *Edwards* rule for the Fifth Amendment, such a waiver of the Sixth Amendment right to counsel will likely be upheld as valid.

---

608 *Montejo*, 556 U.S. at 789.

609 State v. Montejo, 40 So. 3d 952, 957 (La.), *cert. denied*, 562 U.S. 1082 (2010).

3. Remedies for Violations of the Sixth Amendment Right to Counsel

Violations of the Sixth Amendment right to counsel in the interrogation context are treated in much the same way *Miranda* violations are treated. Thus, any incriminating statements made by a defendant that are obtained in violation of the Sixth Amendment are inadmissible at trial in the prosecution's case-in-chief.[610] But so long as statements obtained in violation of the Sixth Amendment were voluntary (i.e., due process was not also violated), then statements are admissible under one of two circumstances: (1) if necessary to show inconsistencies in a defendant's statement for impeachment or perjury purposes; and (2) if one of the exceptions to the exclusionary rule applies (e.g., good faith, attenuation, etc.).[611]

4. Subsequent Waiver After Initial Violation of the Sixth Amendment

Recall that, under *Oregon v. Elstad*, if suspects being subjected to custodial interrogation make incriminating statements without having been given *Miranda* rights, subsequent reiterations of those incriminating statements after a proper administration of *Miranda* warnings can purge the taint of the initial constitutional violation so long as the initial statements were knowingly and voluntarily given.[612] Thus, *Elstad* held that the fruit of the poisonous tree doctrine applies only if the initial *Miranda* violation was accompanied by deliberately coercive or improper tactics in obtaining the initial statement. Although the U.S. Supreme Court has not yet ruled on whether the *Elstad* would similarly disallow the fruit of the poisonous tree doctrine to Sixth Amendment violations, at least one U.S. Circuit Court of Appeals has extended *Elstad* to the Sixth Amendment realm.

As previously explained, the U.S. Supreme Court determined in *Fellers v. United States* that post-indictment statements made by a

---

[610] Michigan v. Harvey, 494 U.S. 344 (1990).

[611] Kansas v. Ventris, 556 U.S. 586 (2009).

[612] Oregon v. Elstad,470 U.S. 298 (1985).

defendant in response to police statements while being arrested on methamphetamine charges violated the defendant's Sixth Amendment right to counsel.[613] The Court ended its decision in *Fellers* by remanding the case for consideration of the question of whether the Sixth Amendment required suppression of Feller's "jailhouse statements on the ground that they were the fruits of previous questioning conducted in violation of the Sixth Amendment deliberate-elicitation standard."[614] On remand, the Eighth Circuit answered that question in the negative:[615]

> In contrast with the statements made at Fellers's home, Fellers's jailhouse statements were given after a proper administration of *Miranda* warnings and a proper oral and written waiver of his *Miranda* rights. The *Miranda* warnings fully informed Fellers of "the sum and substance" of his Sixth Amendment rights, and his waiver of his *Miranda* rights operated as a knowing, intelligent, and voluntary waiver of his right to counsel [under *Patterson*] . . . . He was thus given all of the information he needed to decide whether to invoke his Sixth Amendment rights. Furthermore, no evidence indicates that either Fellers's initial statements or his subsequent jailhouse statements were coerced, compelled, or otherwise involuntary. As a result, the condition that made his prior statements inadmissible—the inability to have counsel present or to waive the right to counsel—was removed.[616]

---

[613] Fellers v. United States, 540 U.S. 519 (2004).

[614] *Id.* at 525.

[615] United States v. Fellers, 397 F.3d 1090 (8th Cir. 2005), *abrogated on other grounds as recognized by* United States v. Thorpe, 477 F.3d10 565 (8th Cir. 2006).

[616] *Id.* at 1097 (internal citations omitted).

Chapter 11:

Conclusion

A. Summary of "Black Letter Law"

An admission or confession obtained by a law enforcement officer is inadmissible in court unless (1) it is voluntary and (2) the requirements of *Miranda v. Arizona* are satisfied. A statement is involuntary if it is a product of police coercion, whether by force or by subtler forms of coercion, and if, in the totality of the circumstances, the statement is not the result of a person's free and rational choice. In determining voluntariness, courts consider the personal characteristics of the defendant, such as age, mental capacity, physical or mental impairment, and experience with the police, in establishing the setting in which coercion might operate to overcome the defendant's will.

Miranda held that a statement obtained by police during a custodial interrogation of a defendant is inadmissible unless the police used certain procedural safeguards to secure the defendant's privilege against self-incrimination. Those procedural safeguards are (1) giving warnings of rights and (2) obtaining a valid waiver of those rights before an interrogation is begun. Therefore, the major issues of *Miranda* fall into four categories: custody, interrogation, warnings, and waiver.

A person is in custody if there is a formal arrest or restraint on freedom of movement of the degree associated with a formal arrest. Custody is determined by examining, from a reasonable person's point of view, the totality of facts and circumstances surrounding an encounter between a person and law enforcement authorities. These include the place; the time; the presence of family, friends, or other persons; physical restraint; and coercion or domination by the police.

Interrogation refers not only to express questioning but also to any words or actions on the part of law enforcement officers that they should know are reasonably likely to elicit an incriminating response. Nevertheless, clarifying questions, spontaneous questions, and routine questions are not considered to be interrogations for *Miranda* purposes. In addition, volunteered statements are not the product of interrogation and are not subject to the *Miranda* requirements. Multiple attempts at interrogation are permitted after a defendant invokes the right to silence, but the defendant's right to cut off questioning must be scrupulously honored, fresh warnings must be given, and no coercion or other pressures may be employed. If the defendant has invoked the right to counsel, though, then further interrogation without counsel present may only be conducted upon the initiation of the defendant and the waiver of *Miranda* rights.

Miranda warnings must be recited clearly and unhurriedly in a language understood by the suspect. Special care must be taken to carefully explain the meaning of the warnings to immature, illiterate, or impaired persons. *Miranda* requirements apply regardless of the nature or severity of the offense being investigated. *Miranda* does not apply to civil proceedings such as customs procedures, civil commitments, extradition proceedings, and license revocation proceedings.

A person who waives the *Miranda* rights to remain silent and to have an attorney may be questioned. To be effective, a waiver of *Miranda* rights must be voluntary and made with full awareness of both the nature of the right being abandoned and the consequences of the decision to abandon it. Waiver will not be inferred from mere silence but may be expressed by a great variety of words and gestures. If possible, an officer should obtain a written waiver of rights, because a written waiver provides the best evidence of a voluntary and intentional relinquishment of a known right.

After a defendant has been formally charged and has requested counsel, law enforcement authorities are prohibited under the Sixth Amendment from using any methods, however surreptitious or indirect, to elicit incriminating evidence from the defendant in the absence of counsel.

B. Concluding Thoughts

As you no doubt gather from reading about the plethora of rulings in this book, *Miranda* may be the most famous or infamous U.S. Supreme Court decision of all time, depending on one's perspective. As the various majority, plurality, concurring, and dissenting opinions in self-incrimination cases should make clear, even jurists are divided about *Miranda*'s logic and scope. And over the decades since it was decided, courts have whittled down its protections. Consider what three leading legal scholars had to say about *Miranda* at the start of a chapter in their influential treatise on criminal procedure:

> *Miranda*—the legal doctrine—is alive, but in deeply weakened condition. One former member of the Court, years ago, described the case as "twisting slowly in the wind." As demonstrated in this chapter, the *Miranda* of 1966 is not the *Miranda* of the twenty-first century. Professor Yale Kamisar has observed that, with the departure of Earl Warren and other members of his Court, "almost all Court watchers expected the Supreme Court to treat *Miranda* unkindly. They did not have to wait very long." In most regards, *Miranda* has been narrowly interpreted . . . and exceptions to the doctrine have been created, so that much of the case's potential impact for good or ill has been diminished.[617]

Their observations apply with equal force to *Miranda* waivers and, to a lesser degree, to Sixth Amendment protections in the interrogation and confession setting as well.

---

[617] JOSHUA DRESSLER, ALAN C. MICHAELS & RIC SIMMONS, UNDERSTANDING CRIMINAL PROCEDURE: VOLUME 1: INVESTIGATION 466 (8th ed. 2021).

Bibliography

Cases

A.M. v. Butler, 360 F.3d 787 (7th Cir. 2004).. 49

Albritton v. State, 769 So. 2d 438 (Fla. Dist. Ct. App. 2000). 38, 42

Argersinger v. Hamlin, 407 U.S. 25 (1972). 153

Arizona v. Mauro, 481 U.S. 520 (1987). 73, 74, 114

Arizona v. Roberson, 486 U.S. 675 (1988). 108, 110, 111, 114

Arthur v. State, 575 So. 2d 1165 (Ala. Ct. Crim. App. 1990). 62

Ashcraft v. Tennessee, 322 U.S. 143 (1944). 6, 9, 18, 36, 60

Beaty v. Stewart, 303 F.3d 975 (9th Cir. 2002)..................................... 78

Beckwith v. United States, 425 U.S. 341 (1976)............................. 56, 58

Berghuis v. Thompkins, 560 U.S. 370 (2010)............... 38, 123, 124, 125

Berkemer v. McCarty, 468 U.S. 420 (1984). 31, 59

Bies v. Sheldon, 775 F.3d 386, 402 (6th Cir. 2014). 135

Bivins v. State, 642 N.E.2d 928 (Ind. 1994). 97

Black v. State, 820 P.2d 969 (Wyo. 1991). 42

Brady v. United States, 397 U.S. 742 (1970). 153

Bram v. United States, 168 U.S. 532 (1897). 6

Brewer v. Williams, 430 U.S. 387 (1977)........... 152, 155, 156, 157, 163

Brooks v. Florida, 389 U.S. 413 (1967). 35

Brown v. Mississippi, 297 U.S. 278 (1936). 7, 18, 31

Bruner v. People, 156 P.2d 111 (Colo. 1945).. 18

Bryan v. State, 571 A.2d 170 (Del. 1990). 142

Burket v. Angelone, 208 F.3d 172 (4th Cir. 2000). 88

California v. Prysock, 453 U.S. 355 (1981). 94

Canty v. Alabama, 309 U.S. 629 (1940). 8, 18

Carter v. Kentucky, 450 U.S. 288 (1981). 146, 147

Chambers v. Florida, 309 U.S. 227 (1940). 6, 7, 8, 18

Charles v. Smith, 894 F.2d 718 (5th Cir. 1990). 106

Chavez v. Martinez, 538 U.S. 760 (2003). 25, 32, 145

Coleman v. Alabama, 399 U.S. 1 (1970). 153

Coleman v. Thompson, 501 U.S. 722 (1991). 112

Collazo v. Estelle, 940 F.2d 411 (9th Cir. 1991). 38

Colorado v. Connelly, 479 U.S. 157 (1986). 33, 38, 44, 123, 132, 133

Colorado v. Spring, 479 U.S. 564 (1987). 134, 141

Commonwealth v. A Juvenile, 449 N.E.2d 654 (Mass. 1983). 129

Commonwealth v. Cousar, 928 A.2d 1025 (Pa. 2007). 71

Commonwealth v. D'Entremont, 632 N.E.2d 1239 (Mass. App. Ct. 1994). 77

Commonwealth v. DeJesus, 787 A.2d 394 (Pa. 2001), *abrogated on other grounds by* Commonwealth v. Cousar, 928 A.2d 1025 (Pa. 2007). 71

Commonwealth v. Martin, 827 N.E.2d 198 (Mass. 2005) 144

Commonwealth v. Mavredakis, 725 N.E.2d 169 (Mass. 2000). 142

Commonwealth v. Molina, 104 A.3d 430 (2014). 91

Commonwealth v. Wideman, 334 A.2d 594 (Pa. 1975). 97

Connecticut v. Barrett, 479 U.S. 523 (1987). 115, 116, 124, 131

Cook v. Warden, 677 F.3d 1133 (11th Cir. 2012). 85

Culombe v. Connecticut, 367 U.S. 568 (1961). 6

Davis v. North Carolina, 384 U.S. 737 (1966). 36, 60

Davis v. United States, 512 U.S. 452 (1994). 86, 87

Dennis v. State, 990 P.2d 277 (Okla. 1999). 142

Diaz v. Senkowski, 76 F.3d 61 (2d Cir. 1996). 87

Dickerson v. United States, 530 U.S. 428 (2000) 27, 142

Doe v. United States, 487 U.S. 201 (1988). 24

Douglas v. California, 372 U.S. 353 (1963). 154

Drury v. State, 793 A.2d 567 (Md.), *cert. denied*, 537 U.S. 942 (2002). 70, 71

Edwards v. Arizona, 451 U.S. 477 (1981) 106, 107, 117, 164

Escobedo v. Illinois, 378 U.S. 478 (1964) 13, 14, 151

Estelle v. Smith, 451 U.S. 454 (1981). 67, 68

Ex parte J.D.H., 797 So. 2d 1130 (Ala. 2001) 98

Fare v. Michael C., 442 U.S. 707 (1979) 126, 128, 129

Fellers v. United States, 540 U.S. 519 (2004). 151, 159, 160, 168

Florida v. Powell, 559 U.S. 50 (2010). 94

Frazier v. Cupp, 394 U.S. 731 (1969). 40, 41

Gagnon v. Scarpelli, 411 U.S. 778 (1973) 154

Gardner v. Johnson, 247 F.3d 551 (5th Cir. 2001). 69

Gideon v. Wainwright, 372 U.S. 335 (1963) 15, 153

Gilliam v. Sealey, 932 F.3d 216 (4th Cir. 2019). 140

Gore v. Sec'y for Dep't of Corr., 492 F.3d 1273 (11th Cir. 2007) 105

Greenwald v. Wisconsin, 390 U.S. 519 (1968). 36

Griffin v. California, 380 U.S. 609 (1965). 146

Griffin v. Strong, 983 F.2d 1540 (10th Cir. 1993). 34

Haley v. Ohio, 332 U.S. 596 (1944). 6, 9

Hall v. Thomas, 611 F.3d 1259 (11th Cir. 2010). 137

Hamilton v. Alabama, 368 U.S. 52 (1961). 153

Hardaway v. Young, 302 F.3d 757 (7th Cir. 2002). 137

Harris v. Bornhorst, 513 F.3d 503 (6th Cir. 2008). 137

Harris v. New York, 401 U.S. 222 (1971) 25, 142

Hart v. Att'y Gen. of Fla., 323 F.3d 884 (11th Cir. 2003)................... 140

Hendricks v. Vasquez, 974 F.2d 1099 (9th Cir. 1992), *amended sub nom.* Hendricks v. Calderon, 70 F.3d 1032 (9th Cir. 1995)...................... 67

Hopkins v. Cockrell, 325 F.3d 579 (5th Cir. 2003)............................... 43

Howes v. Fields, 565 U.S. 499 (2012).. 48, 55

Illinois v. Perkins, 496 U.S. 292 (1990).. 85, 86

In re B.M.B., 955 P.2d 1302 (Kan. 1998)... 129

In re C.H., 763 N.W.2d 708 (Neb. 2009)... 49

In re C.S.C., 118 P.3d 970 (Wyo. 2005).. 49

In re Durand, 293 N.W.2d 383 (Neb. 1980).. 67

In re E.T.C., 449 A.2d 937 (Vt. 1982)... 129

In re J.F. 987 A.2d 1168 (D.C. 2010);... 49

J.D.B. v. North Carolina, 564 U.S. 261 (2011)........................ 49, 50, 51

Johnson v. State, 721 So. 2d 650 (Miss. Ct. App. 1998)....................... 42

Jones v. State, 119 S.W.3d 766 (Tex. Ct. Crim. App. 2003)................. 98

Kansas v. Ventris, 556 U.S. 586 (2009).. 167

Kastigar v. United States, 406 U.S. 441 (1972).................................... 90

Kier v. State, 132 A.2d 494 (Md. 1957)... 18

Kirby v. Illinois, 406 U.S. 682 (1972)... 153

Koh v. Ustich, 933 F.3d 836 (7th Cir. 2019)... 140

Kuhlmann v. Wilson, 477 U.S. 436 (1986)... 160

Lam v. Kelchner, 304 F.3d 256 (3d Cir. 2002).................................. 34, 41

Ledbetter v. Edwards, 35 F.3d 1062 (6th Cir. 1994).............................. 87

Lewis v. Miller, 220 F.3d 485 (7th Cir. 2000).. 132

Leyra v. Denno, 347 U.S. 556 (1954).. 18

Lisenba v. California, 314 U.S. 219 (1941)... 9

Lomax v. Texas, 313 U.S. 544 (1941).. 8

Mahaffey v. Schomig, 294 F.3d 907 (7th Cir. 2002)............................. 69

Maine v. Moulton, 474 U.S. 159 (1985). 158, 159, 160, 162

Malinski v. New York, 324 U.S. 401 (1945). 9, 18

Malloy v. Hogan, 378 U.S. 1 (1964). 146

Mapp v. Ohio, 367 U.S. 643 (1961). 143

Maryland v. Shatzer, 559 U.S. 98 (2010)............. 55, 108, 111, 112, 113

Mason v. Mitchell, 320 F.3d 604 (6th Cir. 2003)................................ 54

Massiah v. United States, 377 U.S. 201 (1964).......................... 153, 155

McDonald v. City of Chicago, 561 U.S. 742 (2010). 153

McKinney v. Ludwick, 649 F.3d 484 (6th Cir. 2011). 117

McNeil v. Wisconsin, 501 U.S. 171 (1991). 108, 161

Medina v. California, 505 U.S. 437 (1992). 68

Mempa v. Rhay, 389 U.S. 128 (1967). 154

Michigan v. Harvey, 494 U.S. 344 (1990). 142, 167

Michigan v. Jackson, 475 U.S. 625 (1986). 165

Michigan v. Mosley, 423 U.S. 96 (1975). 104, 105, 111

Michigan v. Summers, 452 U.S. 692 (1981)... 61

Michigan v. Tucker, 417 U.S. 433 (1974). 100, 144

Mincey v. Arizona, 437 U.S. 385 (1978). 35, 138

Minnesota v. Murphy, 465 U.S. 420 (1984). 60

Minnick v. Mississippi, 498 U.S. 146 (1990)...................... 108, 109, 110

Minnick v. State, 551 So. 2d 77 (Miss. 1988), *rev'd*, 498 U.S. 146 (1990). 109

Miranda v. Arizona, 384 U.S. 436 (1966)... 1, 2, 6, 17, 18, 20, 21, 23, 24, 47, 48, 54, 60, 78, 93, 94, 100, 104, 109, 119, 122, 132, 153

Missouri v. Frye, 566 U.S. 134 (2012). 153

Missouri v. Seibert, 542 U.S. 600 (2004). 102, 103, 144

Mitchell v. United States, 526 U.S. 314 (1999). 148

Montejo v. Louisiana, 556 U.S. 778 (2009). 164, 165, 166

Moran v. Burbine, 475 U.S. 412 (1986)............. 103, 129, 132, 133, 141

Morrissey v. Brewer, 408 U.S. 471 (1972). 154

Murray v. Earle, 405 F.3d 278 (5th Cir. 2005).. 49

Nelson v. Fulcomer, 911 F.2d 928 (3d Cir. 1990)................................ 72

New York v. Quarles, 467 U.S. 649 (1984). 26, 31, 82, 83

Nguyen v. Garcia, 477 F.3d 716 (9th Cir. 2007).................................. 68

North Carolina v. Butler, 441 U.S. 369 (1979). 121, 124, 140

Oregon v. Bradshaw, 462 U.S. 1039 (1983). 117, 130

Oregon v. Elstad, 470 U.S. 298 (1993). 25, 68, 99, 100, 101, 116, 144, 167

Oregon v. Hass, 420 U.S. 714 (1975).. 142

Orozco v. Texas, 394 U.S. 324 (1969). 56, 59

Parsad v. Greiner, 337 F.3d 175 (2d Cir. 2003). 54

Patterson v. Illinois, 487 U.S. 285 (1988). 152, 163, 164

Pennsylvania v. Bruder, 488 U.S. 9 (1988)... 59

Pennsylvania v. Muniz, 496 U.S. 582 (1990)........................... 25, 80, 81

Penry v. Johnson, 215 F.3d 504 (5th Cir. 2000), *rev'd on other grounds*, 532 U.S. 782 (2001). 67

People v. Bender, 551 N.W.2d 71 (Mich. 1996)................................ 142

People v. Bernasco, 541 N.E.2d 774 (Ill. App. Ct. 1989), *aff'd*, 562 N.E.2d 958 (Ill. 1990)... 45, 46

People v. Braggs, 810 N.E.2d 472 (Ill. 2004) 49

People v. Butterfield, 65 Cal. Rptr. 765 (Cal. App. 1968). 60

People v. Jenkins, 268 N.E.2d 198 (Ill. App. Ct. 1971). 78

People v. Keene, 539 N.Y.S.2d 214 (App. Div. 1989)......................... 42

People v. Matlock, 336 P.2d 505 (Cal. 1959).. 18

People v. McCauley, 645 N.E.2d 923 (Ill. 1994). 142

People v. McIntyre, 789 P.2d 1108 (Colo. 1990)................................. 42

People v. Milhollin, 751 P.2d 43 (Colo.1988)...................................... 55

People v. Morse, 76 Cal. Rptr. 391, 452 P.2d 607 (Cal. 1969). 81, 82

People v. Portelli, 205 N.E.2d 857 (N.Y. 1965). 18

People v. Quicke, 455 P.2d 787 (Cal. 1969). 82

People v. Savage, 242 N.E.2d 446 (Ill. App. Ct. 1968). 79

People v. Smith, 246 N.E.2d 689 (Ill. App. Ct. 1969). 129

People v. Thomas, 839 P.2d 1174 (Colo. 1992). 42

People v. Wakat, 114 N.E.2d 706 (Ill. 1953). 18

Peoples v. Campbell, 377 F.3d 1208 (11th Cir. 2004). 54

Perkins v. Herbert, 596 F.3d 161 (2d Cir. 2010). 106

Procunier v. Atchley, 400 U.S. 446 (1971). 44

Ragland v. Commonwealth, 191 S.W.3d 569 (Ky. 2006). 126

Reinert v. Larkins, 379 F.3d 76 (3d Cir. 2004). 139

Rhode Island v. Innis, 446 U.S. 291 (1980). 64, 65, 66, 67, 69, 85

Rivera v. Thompson, 879 F.3d 7 (1st Cir. 2018). 52

Rodriguez v. McDonald, 872 F.3d 908 (9th Cir. 2017). 37, 38

Rogers v. Richmond, 365 U.S. 534 (1961). 9

Rosen v. Superintendent Mahanoy SCI, 972 F.3d 245 (3d Cir. 2020)... 67

Ross v. Moffitt, 417 U.S. 600 (1974). 154

Roth v. State, 788 A.2d 101 (Del. 2001). 72

Rothgery v. Gillespie Cnty., 554 U.S. 191 (2008). 153

Saleh v. Fleming, 512 F.3d 548 (9th Cir. 2008). 63

Salinas v. Texas, 570 U.S. 178 (2013). 89, 90, 91

Schmerber v. California, 384 U.S. 757 (1966). 24

Silverthorne Lumber Co. v. United States, 251 U.S. 385 (1920). 143

Smith v. Illinois, 469 U.S. 91 (1984). 88, 112, 124

Smith v. Mullin, 379 F.3d 919 (10th Cir. 2004). 135

Smith v. State, 787 P.2d 1038 (Alaska Ct. App. 1990). 42

Soffar v. Cockrell, 300 F.3d 588 (5th Cir. 2002). 125

South Dakota v. Neville, 459 U.S. 553 (1983).. 80

Sprosty v. Buchler, 79 F.3d 635 (7th Cir.), *cert. denied*, 519 U.S. 854 (1996). 57

Stansbury v. California, 511 U.S. 318 (1994). 49, 51, 59

State v. Alexander, 347 So. 3d 608 (La. 2020). 141

State v. Baker, 521 S.E.2d 2 (Ga. Ct. App. 1999). 42

State v. Bell, 745 S.W.2d 858 (Tenn. 1988)... 131

State v. Bragg, 48 A.3d 769 (Me. 2012).. 71

State v. Brammeier, 464 P.2d 717 (Or. Ct. App. 1970). 126

State v. Cayward, 552 So. 2d 971 (Fla. Dist. Ct. App. 1989)................ 44

State v. Chavarria, 33 P.3d 922 (N.M. Ct. App. 2001). 34, 42

State v. Corns, 426 S.E.2d 324 (S.C. Ct. App. 1992)........................... 42

State v. DeWeese, 582 S.E.2d 786 (W. Va. 2003). 98

State v. Edwards, 338 S.E.2d 126 (N.C. Ct. App. 1985)....................... 42

State v. Elstad, 658 P.2d 552 (Or. Ct. App. 1983), *rev'd*, 480 U.S. 298 (1985). 100

State v. Foster, 729 P.2d 599 (Or. Ct. App. 1986). 42

State v. Horwitz, 191 So. 3d 429 (Fla. 2016). 91

State v. Jones, 607 S.E.2d 498 (W. Va. 2004)............................ 131, 132

State v. Knapp, 700 N.W.2d 899 (Wis. 2005)...................................... 144

State v. Lescard, 517 A.2d 1158 (N.H. 1986) 55

State v. McAdams, 193 So. 3d 824 (Fla. 2016).................................. 141

State v. Montejo, 40 So. 3d 952 (La.), *cert. denied*, 562 U.S. 1082 (2010). 166

State v. Murphy, 747 N.E.2d 765 (Ohio 2001). 125

State v. Owen, 510 N.W.2d 503 (Neb. Ct. App. 1993). 62

State v. Patton, 826 A.2d 783 (N.J. Super. App. Div. 2003)................. 43

State v. Phelps, 456 N.W.2d 290 (Neb. 1990)................................. 34, 42

State v. Pilcher, 472 N.W.2d 327 (Minn. 1991). 42

State v. Pontbriand, 878 A.2d 227 (Vt. 2005). 55

State v. Porter, 281 S.E.2d 377 (N.C. 1981). 79

State v. Presha, 748 A.2d 1108 (N.J. 2000). 129

State v. Reed, 627 A.2d 630 (N.J. 1993). 142

State v. Rees, 748 A.2d 976 (Me. 2000). 44, 45

State v. Ritter, 485 S.E.2d 492 (Ga. 1997). 43

State v. Roache, 803 A.2d 572 (N.H. 2002). 141

State v. Schumacher, 37 P.3d 6 (Idaho Ct. App. 2001). 40

State v. Simonsen, 878 P.2d 409 (Or. 1994). 142

State v. Stephenson, 915 A.2d 327 (Conn. Ct. App. 2007). 121

State v. Stoddard, 537 A.2d 446 (Conn. 1988). 142

State v. Strayhand, 911 P.2d 577 (Ariz. Ct. App. 1995). 42

State v. Sudduth, No. 93,633, 2006 WL 90102 (Kan. Ct. App. Jan. 13, 2006). 32

State v. Tuttle, 650 N.W.2d 20 (S.D. 2002). 34, 42

State v. Uganiza, 702 P.2d 1352 (Haw. 1985). 71

State v. Wright, 587 N.E.2d 906 (Ohio Ct. App. 1990). 35, 42

Stein v. New York, 346 U.S. 156 (1953). 6

Subdiaz-Osorio v. Humphreys, 947 F.3d 434 (7th Cir. 2020). 88

Texas v. Cobb, 532 U.S. 162 (2001). 162

Thai v. Mapes, 412 F.3d 970 (8th Cir. 2005). 140

Thompson v. Keohane, 516 U.S. 99 (1995), *superseded on other grounds by statute*, 28 U.S.C. § 2254(d). 47

Thompson v. State, 235 So. 2d 354 (Fla. Dist. Ct. App. 1970). 125

Tice v. Johnson, 647 F.3d 87 (4th Cir. 2011). 87

Tollett v. Henderson, 411 U.S. 258 (1973). 153

Townsend v. Sain, 372 U.S. 293 (1963). 33

United States *ex rel.* Henne v. Fike, 563 F.2d 809 (7th Cir.1977), *cert. denied*, 434 U.S. 1072 (1978). 96

United States v. A.R., 38 F.3d 699 (3d Cir. 1994). 68

United States v. Abdallah, 911 F.3d 201 (4th Cir. 2018). 87, 106

United States v. Alexander, 447 F.3d 1290 (10th Cir. 2006). 75

United States v. Anderson, 929 F.2d 96 (2d Cir. 1991). 69, 138

United States v. Azua-Rinconda, 914 F.3d 319 (4th Cir. 2019)............ 60

United States v. Bailey, 743 F.3d 322 (2d Cir. 2014). 51

United States v. Ballard, 586 F.2d 1060 (5th Cir. 1978). 33

United States v. Barnes, 713 F.3d 1200 (9th Cir. 2013)......................... 61

United States v. Basher, 629 F.3d 1161 (9th Cir. 2011)......................... 84

United States v. Bautista-Avila, 6 F.3d 1360 (9th Cir. 1993). 135

United States v. Bengivenga, 845 F.2d 593 (5th Cir. 1988)................... 48

United States v. Benton, 996 F.2d 642 (3d Cir. 1993). 71

United States v. Beraun-Panez, 812 F.2d 578 (9th Cir. 1987). 63

United States v. Bezanson-Perkins, 390 F.3d 34 (1st Cir. 2004). 87

United States v. Borchardt, 809 F.2d 1115 (5th Cir. 1987)................... 84

United States v. Boykin, 398 F.2d 483 (3d Cir. 1968). 125

United States v. Briggs, 273 F.3d 737 (7th Cir. 2001).......................... 73

United States v. Cardwell, 433 F.3d 378 (4th Cir. 2005). 126

United States v. Carpentino, 948 F.3d 10 (1st Cir. 2020). 139

United States v. Castro-Higuero, 473 F.3d 880 (8th Cir. 2007). 125

United States v. Cavazos, 668 F.3d 190 (5th Cir. 2012). 56

United States v. Cazares, 788 F.3d 956 (9th Cir. 2015). 63

United States v. Chamberlain, 163 F.3d 499 (8th Cir. 1998). 55

United States v. Chancellor, No. 07-20578-CR, 2008 WL 622937 (S.D. Fla. Feb. 8, 2008)... 32

United States v. Cheely, 36 F.3d 1439 (9th Cir. 1994). 55

United States v. Clenney, 631 F.3d 658 (4th Cir. 2011). 24

United States v. Coonce, 932 F.3d 623 (8th Cir. 2019). 67

United States v. Cristobal, 293 F.3d 134 (4th Cir. 2002). 139

United States v. Delaney, 443 F. App'x 122 (6th Cir. 2011). 87

United States v. DeMarce, 564 F.3d 989 (8th Cir. 2009). 105

United States v. Dionisio, 410 U.S. 1 (1973). 25

United States v. Drapeau, 414 F.3d 869 (8th Cir. 2005). 89

United States v. Elliott, 876 F.3d 855 (6th Cir. 2017). 57

United States v. Ellison, 632 F.3d 727 (1st Cir. 2010). 55

United States v. Farinacci-Garcia, 551 F. Supp. 465 (D.P.R. 1982). 93

United States v. Fellers, 397 F.3d 1090 (8th Cir. 2005), *abrogated on other grounds as recognized by* United States v. Thorpe, 477 F.3d10 565 (8th Cir. 2006). 168

United States v. Ferrer-Montoya, 483 F.3d 565 (8th Cir. 2007). 98

United States v. Fouche, 833 F.2d 1284 (9th Cir. 1987), cert denied, 486 U.S. 1017 (1988). 87

United States v. Frankson, 83 F.3d 79 (4th Cir. 1996). 96

United States v. Frazier, 476 F.2d 891 (D.C. Cir. 1973). 131

United States v. Giddins, 858 F.3d 870 (4th Cir. 2017). 42, 52

United States v. Gonzalez-Sandoval, 894 F.2d 1043 (9th Cir. 1990). ... 81

United States v. Griffin, 922 F.2d 1343 (8th Cir. 1990). 60

United States v. Guarno, 819 F.2d 28 (2d Cir. 1987). 36, 39

United States v. Hashime, 734 F.3d 278 (4th Cir. 2013). 56, 61

United States v. Henley, 984 F.2d 1040 (9th Cir. 1993). 81

United States v. Henry, 447 U.S. 264 (1980). 154, 157, 158

United States v. Higgins-Vogt, 911 F.3d 814 (7th Cir. 2018). 37

United States v. Hodge, 714 F.3d 380 (6th Cir. 2013). 84

United States v. Horton, 490 F. Supp. 2d 1161 (D. Kan. 2007). 54

United States v. Hunter, 708 F.3d 938 (7th Cir. 2013). 88

United States v. Ivy, 929 F.2d 147 (5th Cir. 1991). 115

United States v. Jackson, 544 F.3d 351 (1st Cir. 2008). 84

United States v. Jackson, No. 1:08CR00076SNLJ, 2010 WL 254927 (E.D. Mo. Jan. 19, 2010). 32

United States v. Jacques, 744 F.3d 804 (1st Cir. 2014). 137

United States v. Jonas, 786 F.2d 1019 (11th Cir. 1986). 63

United States v. Jones, 147 F. Supp. 2d 752 (E.D. Mich. 2001). 96

United States v. Juvenile Male, 554 F.3d 456 (4th Cir. 2009). 68

United States v. Khalil, 214 F.3d 111 (2d Cir. 2000). 138

United States v. Kim, 292 F.3d 969 (9th Cir. 2002). 61, 62

United States v. Kimbrough, 477 F.3d 144 (4th Cir. 2007). 84, 85

United States v. Koch, 552 F.2d 1216 (7th Cir. 1977). 35

United States v. Kourani, 6 F.4th 345 (2d Cir. 2021). 36

United States v. LaBare, 191 F.3d 60 (1st Cir. 1999). 160

United States v. Lall, 607 F.3d 1277 (11th Cir. 2010). 38, 43

United States v. Lim, 897 F.3d 673 (5th Cir. 2018). 84

United States v. Mack, No. 07-238, 2009 WL 580430 (M.D. La. Mar. 6, 2009). 32

United States v. Madoch, 149 F.3d 596 (7th Cir. 1998). 56

United States v. Martin, 664 F.3d 684 (7th Cir. 2011). 117

United States v. Mashburn, 406 F.3d 303 (4th Cir. 2005). 34, 42

United States v. Mays, 683 F. App'x 427 (6th Cir. 2017). 87

United States v. McClinton, 982 F.2d 278 (8th Cir. 1992). 37

United States v. Melo, 954 F.3d 334 (1st Cir. 2020). 56

United States v. Menzer, 29 F.3d 1223 (7th Cir. 1994). 55

United States v. Mittel-Carey, 493 F.3d 36 (1st Cir. 2007). 56, 59

United States v. Mobley, 40 F.3d 688 (4th Cir. 1994). 83, 84

United States v. Morgan, 738 F.3d 1002 (9th Cir. 2013). 39

United States v. Oliver, 630 F.3d 397 (5th Cir. 2011). 121

United States v. Outland, 993 F.3d 1017 (7th Cir. 2021). 139

United States v. Pacheco-Lopez, 531 F.3d 420 (6th Cir. 2008). 81

United States v. Padilla, 387 F.3d 1087 (9th Cir. 2004)........................ 69

United States v. Palmer, 203 F.3d 55 (1st Cir. 2000). 137

United States v. Parra, 2 F.3d 1058 (10th Cir. 1993). 81

United States v. Patane, 542 U.S. 630 (2004). 26, 144

United States v. Patterson, No. 3:09-cr-7(S1)-J-32TEM, 2009 WL 10670083 (M.D. Fla. June 22, 2009)... 32

United States v. Plugh, 648 F.3d 118 (2d Cir. 2011). 88

United States v. Plumman, 409 F.3d 919 (8th Cir. 2005). 51

United States v. Preston, 751 F.3d 1008 (9th Cir. 2014)..................... 135

United States v. Pruden, 398 F.3d 241 (3rd Cir.2005). 96

United States v. Quinn, 815 F.2d 153 (1st Cir. 1987). 57

United States v. Rambo, 365 F.3d 906 (10th Cir. 2004). 70, 77

United States v. Rang, 919 F.3d 113 (1st Cir. 2019). 136

United States v. Reynolds, 367 F.3d 294 (5th Cir. 2004).................... 139

United States v. Robinson, 404 F.3d 850 (4th Cir. 2005). 135

United States v. Rodriguez-Preciado, 399 F.3d 1118 (9th Cir. 2005).... 95

United States v. Rogers, 906 F.2d 189 (5th Cir. 1990). 38

United States v. Romero, 897 F.2d 47 (2d Cir. 1990). 84

United States v. Rouse, No. 4:09-CR-21-FL2, 2009 WL 2602347 (E.D.N.C. Aug. 21, 2009)... 96

United States v. Saadeh, 61 F.3d 510 (7th Cir. 1995). 61

United States v. Sablotny, 21 F.3d 747 (7th Cir. 1994). 39, 40

United States v. Sanchez, 614 F.3d 876 (8th Cir. 2010). 39

United States v. Scott, 270 F.3d 30 (1st Cir. 2001). 79

United States v. Simpkins, 978 F.3d 1 (1st Cir. 2020). 84

United States v. Slaight, 620 F.3d 816 (7th Cir. 2010). 54

United States v. Steele, 648 F. Supp. 1375 (N.D. Ind. 1986). 57

United States v. Street, 472 F.3d 1298 (11th Cir. 2006). 93
United States v. Swan, 842 F.3d 28 (1st Cir. 2016). 36, 54
United States v. Taylor, 745 F.3d 15 (2d Cir. 2014). 138
United States v. Taylor, 985 F.2d 3 (1st Cir. 1993). 73
United States v. Thomas, 11 F.3d 1392 (7th Cir. 1993). 72
United States v. Thorpe, 477 F.3d10 565 (8th Cir. 2006). 168
United States v. Tillman, 963 F.2d 137 (6th Cir. 1992). 95
United States v. Tyler, 164 F.3d 150 (3d Cir. 1998). 70
United States v. Vazquez, 857 F.2d 857 (1st Cir. 1988). 75, 76
United States v. Walker, 272 F.3d 407 (7th Cir. 2001). 139
United States v. Webb, 311 F. App'x 582 (4th Cir. 2009). 96
United States v. Webster, 162 F.3d 308 (5th Cir. 1998). 84
United States v. Williams, 842 F.3d 1143 (9th Cir. 2016). 81
United States v. Wright, 777 F.3d 769 (5th Cir. 2015). 58
United States v. Wright, 991 F.2d 1180 (4th Cir. 1993). 78
United States v. Young, 964 F.3d 938 (10th Cir. 2020). 70
United States v. Younger, 398 F.3d 1179 (9th Cir. 2005). 87
Vega v. Tekoh, 142 S. Ct. 2095 (2022). 145, 146
Vernon v. Alabama, 313 U.S. 547 (1941). 8, 18
Wakat v. Harlib, 253 F.2d 59 (7th Cir. 1958). 18
Ward v. Texas, 316 U.S. 547 (1942). 18
Watkins v. Callahan, 724 F.2d 1038 (1st Cir. 1984). 126
Watson v. Detella, 122 F.3d 450 (7th Cir. 1997). 95
Watts v. Indiana, 338 U.S. 49 (1949). 9, 36
Webb v. State, 756 P.2d 293 (Alaska 1988). 42
Weeks v. United States, 232 U.S. 383 (1914). 143
Welch v. Butler, 835 F.2d 92 (5th Cir. 1988). 39
West v. Commonwealth, 887 S.W.2d 338 (Ky. 1994). 142

White v. Texas, 309 U.S. 631 (1940). 8

White v. Texas, 310 U.S. 530 (1940). 18

White v. Woodall, 572 U.S. 415 (2014). 147, 148

Whitehead v. Cowan, 263 F.3d 708 (7th Cir. 2001). 75

Wilcher v. Hargett, 978 F.2d 872 (5th Cir. 1992). 140

Williams v. State, 825 A.2d 1078 (Md. 2003). 35

Wilson v. Coon, 808 F.2d 688 (8th Cir. 1987). 52

Wolf v. Colorado, 338 U.S. 25 (1949). 143

Wood v. Ercole, 644 F.3d 83 (2d Cir. 2011). 88

Yarborough v. Alvarado, 541 U.S. 652 (2004). 48, 49

Statutes

42 U.S.C. § 1983 144

COLO. REV. STAT. ANN. § 19-2-511. 129

CONN. GEN. STAT. ANN. § 46b-137. 129

MONT. CODE ANN. § 41-5-331 129

N.C. GEN. STAT. ANN. § 7B-2101 129

OKLA. STAT. ANN. tit. 10A, § 2-2-301. 129

Other Authorities

Beyer, Marty, *Immaturity, Culpability, and Competency in Juveniles: A Study of 17 Cases*, 15 CRIM. JUST. 26 (2000). 136

BLACKSTONE, WILLIAM, COMMENTARIES ON THE LAWS OF ENGLAND (1765). 5

Booth, Bates, *Confessions, and Methods Employed in Procuring Them*, 4 S. CALIF. L. REV. 83 (1930). 17

BORCHARD, EDWIN M., CONVICTING THE INNOCENT (1932). 23

Caplan, Gerald M., *Questioning* Miranda, 38 VAND. L. REV. 1417 (1985). 10

Cassell, Paul G., & Bret S. Hayman, *Police Interrogation in the 1990s: An Empirical Study of the Effects of* Miranda, 43 UCLA L. REV. 839 (1996). 119, 120

Cassell, Paul G., & Richard Fowles, *Handcuffing the Cops? A Thirty-Year Perspective on Miranda's Harmful Effects on Law Enforcement*, 50 STAN. L. REV. 1055 (1998). 28, 29

Cassell, Paul G., & Richard Fowles, *Still Handcuffing the Cops? A Review of Fifty Years of Empirical Evidence of Miranda's Harmful Effects on Law Enforcement*, 97 B.U. L. REV. 685 (2017). 28

Cassell, Paul G., Miranda*'s Social Costs: An Empirical Reassessment*, 90 NW. U. L. REV. 387 (1996). 28

Cicchini, Michael D., *The New* Miranda *Warning*, 65 SMU L. REV. 911 (2012). 125

Dawes, Donald M., Jeffrey D. Ho, Andrea S. Vincent, Paul C. Nystrom & Brian E. Driver, *The Neurocognitive Effects of a Conducted Electrical Weapon Compared to High Intensity Interval Training and Alcohol Intoxication: Implications for Miranda and Consent*, 53 J. FORENSIC & LEGAL MED. 51 (2018). 32

Dawes, Donald M., Jeffrey D. Ho, Andrea S. Vincent, Paul C. Nystrom, Johanna C. Moore, Lila W. Steinberg, Anne Marie K. Tilton, Michael A. Brave, Marc S. Berris & James R. Miner, *The Neurocognitive Effects of Simulated Use-of-Force Scenarios*, 10 FORENSIC SCI., MED. & PATHOLOGY 9 (2014). 32

Domanico, Anthony J., Michael D. Cicchini & Lawrence T. White, *Overcoming* Miranda: *A Content Analysis of the* Miranda *Portion of Police Interrogations*, 49 IDAHO L. REV. 1 (2012). 119, 120

Donohue, III, John J., *Did* Miranda *Diminish Police Effectiveness?*, 50 STAN. L. REV. 1147 (1998). 28, 29

DRESSLER, JOSHUA, ALAN C. MICHAELS & RIC SIMMONS, UNDERSTANDING CRIMINAL PROCEDURE: VOLUME 1: INVESTIGATION (8th ed. 2021). 171

Feld, Barry C., *Juveniles' Competence to Exercise* Miranda *Rights: An Empirical Study of Policy and Practice*, 91 MINN. L. REV. 26 (2006). 136

Figner, Bernd, & Elke U. Weber, *Who Takes Risks When and Why? Determinants of Risk Taking*, 20 CURRENT DIRECTIONS IN PSYCH. SCI. 211 (2011). 136

Foote, Caleb, *Law and Police Practice: Safeguards in the Law of Arrest*, 52 NW. U. L. REV. 16 (1957). 17

FRANK, JEROME, & BARBARA FRANK, NOT GUILTY (1957). 23

FRIED, CHARLES, ORDER AND LAW: ARGUING THE REAGAN REVOLUTION—A FIRSTHAND ACCOUNT (1991). 30

Godsey, Mark A., *Rethinking the Involuntary Confession Rule: Toward a Workable Test for Identifying Compelled Self-Incrimination*, 93 CALIF. L. REV. 465, 488 (2005) 7

Goldstein, Naomi E. S., Emily Haney-Caron, Marsha Levick & Danielle Whiteman, *Waving Good-Bye to Waiver: A Developmental Argument Against Youths' Waiver of* Miranda *Rights*, 21 N.Y.U. J. LEGIS. & PUB. POL'Y 1 (2018). 128

Goldstein, Naomi E. Sevin, Lois Oberlander Condie, Rachel Kalbeitzer, Douglas Osman & Jessica L Geier, *Juvenile Offenders'* Miranda *Rights Comprehension and Self-Reported Likelihood of Offering False Confessions*, 10 ASSESSMENT 359 (2003). 136

Griffiths, John, & Richard Ayres, Faculty Note, *A Postscript to the* Miranda *Project, Interrogation of Draft Protesters*, 77 YALE L.J. 395 (1967). 27

Grisso, Thomas, & Carolyn Pomicter, *Interrogation of Juveniles: An Empirical Study of Procedures, Safeguards, and Rights Waiver*, 1 LAW & HUM. BEHAV. 321 (1997). 129, 136

Grisso, Thomas, *Juveniles' Capacities to Waive* Miranda *Rights: An Empirical Analysis*, 68 CALIF. L. REV. 1134 (1980). 129

GRISSO, THOMAS, JUVENILES' WAIVER OF RIGHTS: LEGAL AND PSYCHOLOGICAL COMPETENCE (1981). 136

Hall, Jerome, *The Law of Arrest in Relation to Contemporary Social Problems*, 3 U. CHI. L. REV. 345 (1936). 17

HANNAH, JOHN A., ROBERT G. STOREY, ERWIN N. GRISWOLD, THEODORE M. HESBURGH, ROBERT S. RANKIN & SPOTTSWOOD W. ROBINSON, III, 1961 COMMISSION ON CIVIL RIGHTS REPORT: JUSTICE (1961). 18

INBAU, FRED E., & JOHN E. REID, CRIMINAL INTERROGATION AND CONFESSIONS (1962). 23

INBAU, FRED E., & JOHN E. REID, CRIMINAL INTERROGATION AND CONFESSIONS (2d ed. 1967). 66

INBAU, FRED E., & JOHN E. REID, DETECTION AND CRIMINAL INTERROGATION 185 (3d ed.1953). 23

Kane, Robert J., & Michael D. White, *TASER Exposure and Cognitive Impairment: Implications for Valid* Miranda *Waivers and the Timing of Police Custodial Interrogations*, 15 CRIMINOLOGY & PUB. POL'Y 79 (2015). 32

Kassin, Saul M., & Rebecca J. Norwick, *Why People Waive Their* Miranda *Rights: The Power of Innocence*, 28 LAW & HUM. BEHAV. 211 (2004). 120

Kauper, Paul G., *Judicial Examination of the Accused – A Remedy for the Third Degree*, 30 MICH. L. REV. 1224 (1932). 17

King, Kenneth J., *Waiving Childhood Goodbye: How Juvenile Courts Fail to Protect Children from Unknowing, Unintelligent, and Involuntary Waivers of* Miranda *Rights*, 2006 WIS. L. REV. 431 (2006). 129

Klein, Susan R., *Identifying and (Re)Formulating Prophylactic Rules, Safe Harbors, and Incidental Rights in Constitutional Criminal Procedure*, 99 MICH. L. REV. 1030 (2001). 30

Larson, Kimberly, I*mproving the "Kangaroo Courts": A Proposal for Reform in Evaluating Juveniles' Waiver of* Miranda, 48 VILL. L. REV. 629 (2003). 136

Leiken, Lawrence S., *Police Interrogation in Colorado: The Implementation of* Miranda, 47 DENV. L.J. 1 (1970). 28

Leo, Richard A., *Inside the Interrogation Room*, 86 J. CRIM. L. & CRIMINOLOGY 266 (1996). 120

Leo, Richard A., *The Impact of* Miranda *Revisited*, 86 J. CRIM. L. & CRIMINOLOGY 621 (1996). 26, 27, 28, 29, 30, 119, 120

Marcus, Paul, *It's Not Just About* Miranda*: Determining the Voluntariness of Confessions in Criminal Prosecutions*, 40 VAL. U. L. REV. 601 (2006). 40, 41, 42

Medalie, Richard, Leonard Zeitz & Paul Alexander, *Custodial Police Interrogation in Our Nation's Capital: The Attempt to Implement* Miranda, 66 MICH. L. REV. 1347 (1968).......... 27

MILNER, NEIL A., THE COURT AND LOCAL LAW ENFORCEMENT: THE IMPACT OF *MIRANDA* (1971). 27

Neubauer, David W., *Confessions in Prairie City: Some Causes and Effects*, 65 J. CRIM. L. & CRIMINOLOGY 103 (1974).......... 27

O'HARA, CHARLES E., FUNDAMENTALS OF CRIMINAL INVESTIGATION (1956). 23

Penney, Steven, *Theories of Confession Admissibility: A Historical View*, 25 AM. J. CRIM. L. 309 (1998). 5, 6, 8, 11, 15

Redlich, Allison D., Melissa Silverman & Hans Steiner, *Pre-Adjudicative and Adjudicative Competence in Juveniles and Young Adults*, 21 BEHAV. SCI. & L. 393 (2003). 136

Rogers, Richard, Lisa L. Hazelwood, Kenneth W. Sewell, Hayley L. Blackwood, Jill E. Rogstad & Kimberly S. Harrison, *Development and Initial Validation of the* Miranda *Vocabulary Scale*, 33 LAW & HUM. BEHAV. 381 (2009).......... 136

Ruebner, Ralph, *Police Interrogation: The Privilege Against Self-Incrimination, the Right to Counsel, and the Incomplete Metamorphosis of Justice White*, 48 U. MIAMI L. REV. 511 (1994).. 15

Ryan, Meghan J., *Is* Miranda *Good News or Bad News for the Police? The Usefulness of Empirical Evidence*, 50 TEX. TECH L. REV. 81 (2017). 26, 29

Schulhofer, Stephen J., Miranda*'s Practical Effect: Substantial Benefits and Vanishingly Small Social Costs*, 90 NW. U. L. REV. 500 (1996).28

Schulhofer, Steven J., *Bashing* Miranda *Is Unjustified—and Harmful*, 20 HARV. J.L. & PUB. POL'Y 347 (1997). 28

Seeburger, Richard, & R. Stanton Wettick, Jr., Miranda *in Pittsburgh—A Statistical Study*, 29 U. PITT. L. REV. 1 (1967).......... 27

SKOLNICK, JEROME H., & JAMES J. FYFE, ABOVE THE LAW: POLICE AND THE EXCESSIVE USE OF FORCE (1993). 6

Softley, Paul, *Police Interrogation: An Observational Study in Four Police Stations*, HOME OFF. RSCH UNIT REP. 28 (1980). 120

Swift, Katherine M., *Drawing a Line Between* Terry *and* Miranda: *The Degree and Duration of Restraint*, 73 U. CHI. L. REV. 1075 (2006). 62

Thomas, III, George C., & Richard A. Leo, *The Effects of* Miranda v. Arizona: *"Embedded" in Our National Culture?*, 29 CRIME & JUST. 203 (2002). 28

Thompson, Sandra Guerra, *Evading* Miranda: *How* Seibert *and* Patane *Failed To "Save"* Miranda, 40 VAL. U. L. REV. 645 (2006) 30

Wald, Michael, Richard Ayres, David Hess, Mark Schantz & Charles Whitebread, *Interrogations in New Haven: The Impact of* Miranda, 76 YALE L.J. 1519 (1967). 27

White, Michael D., Justin T. Ready, Robert J. Kane & Lisa M. Dario, *Examining the Effects of the TASER on Cognitive Functioning: Findings from a Pilot Study with Police Recruits*, 10 J. EXPERIMENTAL CRIMINOLOGY 267 (2014) 32

WICKERSHAM, GEORGE W., HENRY W. ANDERSON, NEWTON D. BALCER, ADA L. COMSTOCK, WILLIAM I. GRUBB, WILLIAM S. KENYON, MONTE M. LEMANN, FRANK J. LOESCH, KENNETH MACINTOSH, PAUL J. MCCORMICK & ROSCOE POUND, U.S. NAT'L COMM'N ON LAW OBSERVANCE & ENF'T, PUB. NO. 11, REPORT ON LAWLESSNESS IN LAW ENFORCEMENT (1931) 5, 6, 8, 17

Woolard, Jennifer L., Hayley M.D. Cleary, Samantha A. S. Harvell & Rusan Chen, *Examining Adolescents' and their Parents' Conceptual & Practical Knowledge of Police Interrogation: A Family Dyad Approach*, 37 J. YOUTH & ADOLESCENCE 685 (2008) 129, 136

Younger, Evelle J., *Interrogation of Criminal Defendants—Some Views on* Miranda v. Arizona, 35 FORDHAM L. REV. 255 (1966) 27

Younger, Evelle J., *Results of a Survey Conducted in the District Attorney's Office of Los Angeles County Regarding the Effect of the* Miranda *Decision Upon the Prosecution of Felony Cases*, 5 AM. CRIM. L.Q. 32 (1966). 27

Index

42 U.S.C. § 1983, 144–46

A

admission, 1

C

confession, 2
custodial interrogation, 47
custody, 47–64
 duration of interrogation, 60
 execution of search warrants, 61–62
 focus of the investigation, 58
 juvenile age, 49–51
 language used to summon, 62
 location of encounter, 53–57
 number of officers, 57, 58
 physical restraint, 51–53
 presence of others, 60
 probation/parole, 60
 Terry stops, 59
 time of interrogation, 59

E

exclusionary rule, 142
express waivers, 120

F

focus of the investigation, 13–15
fruit of the poisonous tree doctrine, 143–44

I

implied waivers, 121
incommunicado interrogation, 7, 8, 17, 23, 60
interrogation, 2, 8, 17, 64–86
 appeals to conscience, 70
 clarifying questions, 79
 coached lineups, 66
 evidence of guilt, 70–72
 implying blame, 70
 psychiatric evaluations, 67–69
 questioning by private persons, 84, 85
 questioning by undercover agents, 85, 86
 reverse lineups, 67
 routine booking questions, 79–81
 seeking suspect's cooperation, 69
 spontaneous questions, 81, 82
 volunteered statements, 77, 78
involuntary statements, 7, 10, 32

M

Miranda rights
 ambiguous language, 87, 88
 invoking, 86
 silence without invocation, 89, 90, 91
Miranda warnings, 23, 93–95
 after counsel invoked, 106–17
 after silence invoked, 104–6
 after unwarned admissions, 99–103

manner of administration, 95
timing of initial warnings, 96
timing of subsequent warnings, 97

P

physical force, 31
psychological ploys, 69–77
public safety exception, 26, 31, 83

S

selective waivers, 114, 130–32
Sixth Amendment
attachment, 151–54
deliberate elicitation, 155–60
waivers, 162–68
spontaneous questions, 81, 82
statement, 1

T

testimonial evidence, 24, 25, 71, 144
third degree, 5

V

voluntariness
appeals to religious beliefs, 38
deception, 40–44
denial of food or sleep, 36
denial of necessary medical care, 35
evidence of guilt, 39
inhumane conditions, 35
personal characteristics, 44–46
promises of leniency, 36–38
psychological coercion, 32
repay questioning, 36
threats of violence, 34
unnecessary delays, 35

W

waiver requirements, 132–34
age, 136–37
drug or alcohol use, 139
education, 135
intelligence, 135
justice system familiarity, 137
suspect's physical and mental condition, 138–39
Wickersham Commission, 5, 6, 8, 17

www.ingramcontent.com/pod-product-compliance
Lightning Source LLC
Chambersburg PA
CBHW071031020526
44279CB00023B/424/J
* 9 7 8 1 6 8 0 5 3 3 4 3 9 *